A HOUSEWIFE'S ADVENTURE WITH GOD

JESSIE MCFARLANE AND IRENE HOWAT

There's sweetness, the fragrance of Christ, about my friend. It was this sweetness, this gentle strength of Christ that attracted me immediately to Jessie McFarlane. In the room of women, she stood out – and I wanted to know her. And when I came to know her – I not only loved her but appreciated her and the ministry God has given her.

We have shared ministry together in the knolls of Scotland, the city of York, and the valley of Precept Ministries in Chattanooga, Tennessee. We have prayed together ... ministered together ... laughed together ... and shared many a cup of tea. I have stayed in her home, eaten at her kitchen table, and come to know, love and appreciate her husband Peter. I have witnessed their hearts for the Lord and their steadfast perseverance even in the midst of Jessie's physical difficulties. It is a privilege to recommend a book written by a virtuous woman. I, too, look forward to immersing myself in this account of a 'valiant woman of God' and learning from her example. To God, the Potter of our clay, be the glory.

Kay Arthur

If you are an ordinary person desiring to know what an extraordinary God can do with your life, then you need to read this book.

Sammy Tippit
International Itinerant Evangelist

A HOUSEWIFE'S ADVENTURE WITH GOD

*The Continuing story of Jessie McFarlane
and 'Prayer Chain Ministries'*

JESSIE MCFARLANE AND IRENE HOWAT

CHRISTIAN
FOCUS

Copyright © Jessie McFarlane and Irene Howat 2011

ISBN 978-1-84550-786-2

Reprinted in 2011
This edition is new and revised from its first publication in 2000
by
Christian Focus Publications,
Geanies House, Fearn, Ross-shire,
IV20 1TW, Scotland

www.christianfocus.com

Cover design by Daniel van Straaten

Printed by
Bell and Bain, Glasgow

CONTENTS

Dedication

To Peter

who has been my friend, companion and mentor, and to my beloved family for all their love and care. Above all I give this book to the Lord, to be used to bring him great glory.

Acknowledgements

I wish to express sincere thanks and love to Irene Howat, for her love and encouragement in the editing of this new book. My deep appreciation is also due to my colleagues and fellow pray-ers in Prayer Chain Ministry for their love and support over my twenty-five years of leadership in this wonderful ministry.

Jessie McFarlane

Foreword

I like to think of God sitting on his throne putting together a giant eternal jigsaw puzzle, painstakingly working in all the events and people of Planet Earth. With his perfect finished picture firmly in mind, he meticulously fits big important-looking people and events together with his little nondescript children. Some are so insignificant looking most humans would overlook them.

So was Jessie McFarlane as a poor, often depressed and emotionally abused little girl in Scotland's depression just before World War II. But God saw her potential, faith and longing to serve him – not as a wee little piece of humanity, but what he knew from before the foundation of the world he intended to accomplish through her in his eternal puzzle picture.

The story of her childhood is fascinating. A delightful peek into Scottish life in a one-room-and-a-kitchen sandstone tenement, the games, fun times, food, joys and bare survival are all there. Her mom's inability to express love because of her own childhood was sharply contrasted to her extroverted, but not well, father, playing the pipes, leading church singing and making locomotives to ship all over the world. She yearned for the cuddles which never came, receiving only criticism. The first day she made her mother happy was when, at eleven years of age, she accepted Jesus as her Saviour. A soloist since age five, she finally escaped her horrible restrictions by marrying Peter – her pianist, with whom she had ministered all over Scotland. But, through it all, God was preparing Jessie for an awesome place in his giant jigsaw puzzle.

However, it was her relentless search for God in an ever-deepening prayer life that eventually produced a complete Jeremiah 33:3 life for Jessie.

> Call to me,
> And I will answer you,
> And show you great and mighty things, which you
>   know not.' (AKJV)

As God watched her teenage weeping at three-hour prayer meetings, her faithful weekly prayer triplet praying, arranging the 24-hour prayer clock for the Luis Palau Crusade and much more – he knew he could trust her with his incredibly great and mighty things. God picked her to found, organize and run the Telephone Prayer Chains in the whole United Kingdom, had Jessie and Peter be co-founders of the first National Prayer Breakfast in Scotland, and made her a respected international speaker. Reading Isaiah 41:9, Jessie said she suddenly realized 'God had chosen me? Me? ME? An insignificant housewife from Glasgow.'

My now dearest friend Jessie unknowingly was part of my own United Prayer Ministry board's learning that third part of Jeremiah 33:3. When Jessie requested a Glasgow prayer seminar be tacked onto the end of my first United Kingdom speaking tour in 1981, my board and 24-hour prayer clock fervently 'called unto God' for his strength and power. And 'he did answer' those prayers. However, under Jessie, God soon exploded those first 450 members into their powerful National Chains. But, the awesomeness of the 'great and mighty things' God would do through Jessie that we, or Jessie, never dreamed of are in this wonderful book.

This book has something for everyone. Jessie's spiritual journey is full of biblically sound advice – from feeling a phony to victory – from wanting to throw in the towel to a successful international ministry – from deep suffering to being brought back from the gates of heaven. Read it carefully and prayerfully. It will show you how you can let God turn the hard things in your life into those great and mighty things he already had planned for you too.

Evelyn Christenson

1

Born and born again

Thou straggler into loving arms,
Young climber-up of knees.
(Mary Lamb)

When I awoke on the morning of the 12th January 1987 I had elephants with hobnailed boots doing a fandango in my stomach! What had I let myself in for? Why had I said 'Yes' when I had been invited to speak to the Parliamentary Wives' Fellowship in Westminster in London? Who was I to speak to these women about prayer? I lifted my heart in a silent prayer ... HELP!!!

Another chapter in my adventure with God was about to begin, one that started on 28th April 1933 when I was born to William and Jessie Robertson. I was only another statistic in the books of Glasgow's Rottenrow Hospital, but was in the book written by the Master Creator, 'All the days ordained for me were written in your book before one of them came to be' (Ps. 139:16). My adventure in life had begun, a journey that was to take me down many valleys where dark lessons had to be learned and up many high peaks of opportunity and privilege. But it all started off with a little girl in Glasgow.

'He's coming! He's coming!' I could hear Dad's footsteps on the tenement stair. Any minute now he would appear at the close mouth (the entrance to the communal tenement stairway) to be admired by all our wee friends. 'Dad!' my young sister, Wilma, and I shouted, swelling with pride. There he was, dressed in the full Highland regalia that was the uniform of the St Rollox Pipe Band. His embarrassment was probably equalled only by our pride! How handsome he looked! We had good cause to be proud of Dad's piping. When I was a little girl he was chosen to play the piping solo for Scottish dancers performing in the Royal Albert Hall in London. I didn't know much about the Royal Albert Hall and I had certainly never been to London, but I was proud of Dad and loved him very much. And he loved me and I knew it.

Not only did Dad play the pipes, he also built locomotives. Glasgow's Springburn was, in those days, a solid working class area. The Calais, Cowlairs and Hydepark Works meant nearly full employment for the menfolk. Dad worked in Hydepark, a huge factory which produced locomotives to be shipped to the far corners of the world. It was always a thrill when one was completed. The men who built her watched proudly as she left the sheds. My pals and I looked on excitedly. 'My Dad built that!' I boasted, as we followed the beautiful, shining, brand new locomotive, chrome and paint sparkling as it made its way along the first part of its cobblestoned journey to the Clyde. Some went to India, others to China. I was allowed to go as far as Petershill Road before turning for home. How I longed for Dad to come in for his tea to tell him I had seen his locomotive. I wonder if it ever crossed my childlike mind that anyone else at all was involved in its building.

Our home, 290 Springburn Road, was a room and kitchen in a red sandstone tenement, made up of three landings with three homes on each landing. Our house was above the Co-operative Stores, which was, in turn, made up of the grocery store, the dairy, the butcher and the drapery.

My mother did all her shopping there. Everything was bought on credit and the co-operative system meant that she even earned a dividend. I smile when I see advertisements nowadays for the Co-op Dividend Card! The Bible says, 'there is nothing new under the sun' (Eccles. 1:9). How true that is.

Songs often accompanied games. 'One, two, three, a leerie', I sang, bouncing my ball three times off a wall before throwing it up from under my right leg. 'Four, five, six, a leerie', completed the pattern with the other leg. 'Seven, eight, nine, a leerie, hands behind your back', I concluded with a flourish of hands clapped behind my back before either catching the ball or chasing it as it rolled away.

We skipped throughout the summer. Old bits of broken washing line served as skipping ropes. We skipped on our own, up and down the street, avoiding the cracks on the pavement of course. You did not land on a crack. If a number of us gathered, we skipped together, taking it in turns to ca' (turn) the rope. And if only a couple of us wanted to play there was always a lamp post or drainpipe to which we could tie one end of the rope. True, it was a bit sluggish, but the girl at the other end made up for it by ca'ing just a bit harder.

The pavement served for many a game. Having drawn out a numbered grid on the slabs with a bit of broken crockery, we hopped from one to eight and back, pushing a peever in front of us. If the peever landed on a line we were out and had to wait until everyone else had their turns before we could try again. Peevers varied. A flattish stone would do. But the best peevers of all were empty polish tins. Little shoe polish tins were much sought after. Big furniture polish tins were hard work for wee legs.

If the rain came on we ran for the close, there to play houses or schools. Glasgow closes denoted status. If you lived, as we did, in a tenement with a tiled, or wally, close you were a toff. We were toffs. But how I envied my cousins. I thought they were real toffs because they lived in a council house with a garden. While I thought it must be wonderful to have a garden, I knew it had its disadvantages. I still remember my grandmother sending me out with my cousin Arthur to collect horse droppings from the streets to serve as manure in her garden!

Just as surely as boys played with conkers in the autumn when the chestnuts fell off the trees, so girls' games followed a seasonal pattern too. Scraps, little coloured pictures kept treasured between the pages of a book, were exchanged. Intricate patterns were woven by quick fingers with a yard of string tied into a loop. Why that was called Cat's Cradle I can't imagine. Daisies were dismembered to discover whether 'he loved us or he loved us not'. And there was, of course, no better indication of whether or not a friend liked butter than to hold a buttercup under her chin to see if it reflected yellow on her skin!

Our pleasures were simple as were our expectations. How Wilma and I looked forward to Christmas. Our anticipation was not because we expected big, gaily wrapped parcels to yield surprises. We knew what we would get for Christmas, it was the same every year. What we delighted in was almost that: the familiarity, the predictability of it all. Our Christmas tree was about twelve inches high and artificial. After our mother cleaned the house until it shone, and Wilma and I decorated the little tree, it was given pride of place on the sideboard. And when New Year was over, its tiny baubles were wrapped carefully and packed away to be produced again the following year. The disposable society in which we live today was far away in the future. And what did we get? I can close my eyes and picture our gifts: new pyjamas, an Oor Willie or Broons book – they were standard reading for children in the central belt of Scotland and beyond – and a game.

Our stockings, that early Christmas morning delight, held a half crown, an orange, and, if we were fortunate, some sweets. We did not expect too much and we were not disappointed, quite different from the children today who look for designer sneekers, computers, Wiis and so much more. How times have changed!

While my memory of Christmas is of baubles and the Broons, I knew from my earliest days that it celebrated the birth of the Baby Jesus. My mother and father had both professed faith in Jesus Christ when they were young and from my earliest years I knew about him. I cannot remember a time when I did not have an awareness of God or when Sunday worship was not part of the pattern of my life.

Dad's lovely tenor voice led the worship every Sunday at The Glasgow Foundry Boys Religious Society, which met in Garngad in Glasgow. Both my parents were members there. Mum did not often attend. She stayed at home to make the dinner. But sun, rain, hail or snow, I walked hand in hand with Dad or danced beside him, from our home in Springburn Road, down Castle Street and along Garngad Road to worship God. I suppose it was on one of our walks that I learned from Dad how our church came to have such a long name. In the 1860s, there were young men who could find no employment and who were liable to engage in petty dishonesty which sometimes led to lives of crime. The Foundry Boys Religious Society gave itself the task of finding ways in which these uneducated, undisciplined and often poor youths could become God-fearing, self-respecting citizens. They set up their work in four departments: Religious, Social Reform, Educational and Provident.

It seems to me that the church of those days fulfilled the calling of Jesus as he proclaimed it in the Sermon on the Mount. Christians fed the hungry, clothed the poor and set captives free. In the Old Testament, God showed Isaiah that what he wanted from his people was practical love rather than a system of fasting which 'ends in quarrelling and strife'. 'Is this the kind of fast I have chosen ... to loose the chains of injustice and untie the cords of the yoke, to set the oppressed free and break every yoke? Is it not to share your food with the hungry and to provide the poor wanderer with shelter – when you see the naked, to clothe him, and not to turn away from your own flesh and blood?' (Isa. 58:4-7).

When the Foundry Boys began, the church really related to people. God was seen in practical ways as Christians addressed the many social needs of the day.

Later, the Welfare State took over and the bridges between church and society were quietly drawn up. The church retreated into its Castle of Respectability. I wonder if the decline which has been evident in the church for decades is at least in part the result of its taking refuge in religious activities rather than seeing that practical Christianity involves believers being out in the real world and getting their hands dirty. By the time I attended Foundry Boys, the Social Reform and Educational and Provident Departments were things of the past. Only the Religious Department remained, and it was our church.

My mother's best friend, whom we called Aunt Margaret, ran a children's choir in the Foundry Boys. I attended the choir before I ever attended Hydepark Primary School. God gave me both a natural singing voice and a love of song, and by the age of five I was a regular soloist at Sunday school socials which were held for three nights in a row. The church was packed to capacity as parents, grandparents, aunts and uncles came to see their children sing. It was a wonderful way of relating the gospel.

I look at photographs of myself at that time and both smile and wince. I smile at the fresh-faced little girl, at her pretty, full-skirted taffeta dress with its belt tied in a bow at its back and at the bleached white cotton ankle socks atop highly polished buckled shoes. I wince when I look at my hair. Its curl was not natural and it was achieved by nothing less than a form of torture!

Saturday evenings were dedicated to hair. A sheet of newspaper was laid on the floor and after my hair was washed I was sat upon a chair placed in the centre of the paper. How I hated the eternity that followed as my mother bone-combed my hair, strand by strand or so it felt, in a search for any unwanted wildlife, which if found landed on the newspaper and was hastily dispatched. That done, my ordeal had not yet ended. My hair, divided into fine bunches, was held there with metal grips.

Then a length of warm, damp cloth was wound round each bunch and tied at its bottom end. Hair dryers had not been invented. I dried my hair by toasting myself in front of the fire in the living room, turning from side to side when I could bear the heat and the position no longer. The cloths were left in overnight and unwound in the morning. Then came the brushing out ... a tugging, irritating start to a Sunday morning. And all this was for the sake of a curl in my hair that was tied, as fashion demanded at the time, with a bow on one side.

There was nothing of boring duty in my childhood attendance at Foundry Boys. It was fantastic! In those days the hall was packed full for the morning service, which was rather like a Sunday school for children and young people although it was attended by parents and others too. There was lots of singing, enthusiastically led by my father. The choir and junior choir contributed to the praise as did solo singers, my tiny self among them. We always had a speaker who brought God's Word alive in such a way that even a child could begin to understand it. I look back with gratitude on those days and thank God for such a lively start to my Christian upbringing.

Foundry Boys was a focus in our family life, but it was a focus which excluded my mother. She was not happy within that fellowship and when Wilma, who is five years my junior, was old enough to join Dad and me on Sunday mornings, she attended the local Church of Scotland. My sister and I went to the Girls' Brigade Company and the Brownie Pack that met in the Church of Scotland hall, but our church was the Foundry Boys.

Some Saturdays were special. The four of us went away for the day. Our destination was normally one of the Clyde coast towns, Helensburgh being a favourite. Our sense of adventure was all the more because we travelled by train. After walking along the seashore and window-shopping in the town, we took ourselves to a tea room for tea and cakes. What a treat! I wonder if a can of coke in a cafe can ever bring the same feeling of delight as a visit to a tea room in the days just preceding the outbreak of the Second World War.

And there were holidays too. Our mother was a prudent woman, saving her Co-operative dividend all year in order to take a house for a month each summer in Saltcoats. As Dad only had two weeks holiday, we spent the first two weeks of our break without him. The simple pleasures of the seaside were ours. We built sandcastles, topping them with gulls' feathers, and then watched as the incoming tide eroded their foundations and then washed them away. We paddled and played in the sea, dressed in rucked swimsuits that drank in the seawater and slipped down our bodies as they grew heavier and ever heavier. They took ages to dry, sometimes not even completing the process overnight, so that when we put them on the next day the chill made us shudder. But that was nothing to the shudder when we went into the sea.

The Gulf Stream may heat up the sea off the west coast of Scotland, but it doesn't feel like it when you first go into the water! We counted the days till Dad would join us. And when the great day came we counted the hours, then the minutes, till we met him off his train. Dad was the love of our young lives, and the joy of our holiday was complete when he arrived.

As girls, Wilma and I had our treats but we were children of our time. The Depression was happening all around us and money was scarce. For two years during the Depression Dad had no work. Every penny had to earn a pennyworth. Dad's health made matters more difficult. He suffered from emphysema, a dreadful lung condition which caused shortness of breath. Modern bronchodilators had not been invented and Dad's chest became more and more barrel-shaped with the damage to his lungs and the sheer effort of breathing. Every winter he was off work as colds became chest infections and his emphysema played up. Dad was not a complaining man, and he lived with his health problems in a way that was an example to Wilma and me.

Mum's nature was very different from Dad's. He was an extrovert, she an introvert. He loved us and told us so, if not in so many words then in the way he obviously enjoyed our company. Mum loved us too, but she showed it in ways that were difficult for me as a child to recognise as love. Her love was expressed in dusting and cleaning, ironing and mending, in being a capable housewife and in making ends meet. She was not the kind of woman who was comfortable with her children on her knee. Mum's was an efficient love rather than a warm one. I yearned for the warmth and comfort of cuddles. But they never came.

Because of Mum's inability to express her love she seemed to find an outlet in frustration. And unfortunately, as a little girl, I was often the brunt of it. It made her quick-tempered and impulsive, especially with regard to discipline. The expression 'punish first, question later' might have been coined for Mum. Only she often forgot to question, even afterwards. It is a hard conclusion to draw, but I think my childhood relationship with Mum was perhaps one of distant respect on good days, and fear on bad ones.

The date 11th July 1944 is a day I will always remember because it was the day I gave my life to Jesus and asked him to be my Saviour. But I remember it for another reason too. That day, when I was eleven years old, I made my mother happy. We were in Saltcoats and Dad had just joined us. The Scottish Evangelistic Council held a summer mission each year in the town and I loved to go to its children's meetings. Some friends, also from Springburn and holidaying in Saltcoats, went with me. That year, Rev. Austin Stirling of Dunfermline Baptist Church was the leader. On the day of my conversion Christie Gunn preached on, 'For God so loved the world that he gave his only begotten Son, that whosoever believeth in him should not perish, but have everlasting life' (John 3:16, AV). While I already knew the verse off by heart, the concept of God loving the world meant nothing to me. But when Christie asked us to put our own names in place of 'the world' and 'whosoever' it made all the difference. The impact was tremendous. 'For God so loved Jessie Robertson, that if Jessie Robertson believes in him, Jessie Robertson will not perish, but have everlasting life!' God so loved

ME! When an invitation was made for any who wanted to give their lives to Jesus to move to the front of the meeting, I went, along with my three friends.

We laughed and giggled our way to the front. I'm sure Christie Gunn thought we were just frivolous kids. But God had begun a work in my life which he is still completing today. I don't know if my friends' experiences were real, but I know it was real for me.

I went straight back to the place we were staying and told Dad and Mum. They were so pleased. I think Mum felt relief that I was on the right road. Perhaps she also felt a little easing of the weight of responsibility she carried so dutifully on my behalf. Although I was not at ease with my mother, I was aware of her Christian concern for my sister and myself. I knew she prayed for us, and that day, in the grace of God, she saw her prayers answered in my life.

These beach missions dealt with the great issues of eternal life and death. But they were also good fun. Most of the team members were young men at university. I remember them still: Ernest Watson, Tom Houston, John Moore and others. We called them 'uncles'. Sandcastle competitions, games and races were the order of the day. There was more serious stuff too. I won a Bible for quoting a verse of Scripture for every letter of the alphabet, and a book for reciting the whole of Isaiah 53.

I read my Bible as a child, but not in an organised way. These games made me more diligent in my reading. My mother encouraged me too. Although she was not walking closely with the Lord, she knew the path in which she wanted us to walk.

2

Teenage traumas

O memory! thou soul of joy and pain.
(R. Savage)

The Bible tells us that, '[There is] a time to be silent and a time to speak' (Eccles. 3:7). Today there is a vogue for exposing the deepest of feelings, regardless of who will be hurt in the doing of it. It is a pity that it has come to be so, for hurt piled on hurt relieves no-one at all. But the time does come to speak, and my time to tell of my relationship with my mother has come. There is nobody left alive to be hurt by it. And there are many lessons to be learned.

I write from a heart of love because I now understand my mother's problems. When I was a teenager I did not. It was only in the last year of her life that Mother shared her childhood with me. Her mother was a loving woman, loving, that was, to her three sons. She cherished them and showered all her affection on them. Mother figured nowhere in the equation. Starved of love she withdrew from any need of it. And having withdrawn herself as a child, she had no means of accessing that part of herself in adult life. Mother was a clever woman. She worked in a pharmacy, doing dispensing. She was a grafter.

Having lived with criticism my mother became an accomplished critic. She had never learned the power of encouragement. I felt beaten down when my best efforts were seen to be of no value. If I did the ironing it was done again properly. When I polished the furniture, Mother did it all again the right way. And if I tried to avoid such humiliation by not helping with the work I was harangued for that too. There was no way I could win and I felt every bit the loser. In the face of any criticism I immediately apologised. Without considering the rights and wrongs of a situation I accepted I was to blame. 'I'm sorry', peppered my conversation for over forty years, so ingrained did the habit become.

Mother suffered badly from depression. I think she struggled with it all her life. Today she would have been treated. Sometimes I arrived home from school not knowing what lay before me. Often it was a note on the table saying that Dad's dinner was in the oven. We would not know how Mum was, where she was or whether she would return home. She was so very depressed. Sadly, Mother was her own worst enemy.

Her nature and her illness combined to prevent Mother from grasping opportunities to make life easier for herself. When my grandmother died she left Mum £400. I was very young at the time and that was still a lot of money. She could have bought a bungalow in a nice part of the city. It would have eased the pressure on Dad's pay and saved her the climb up and down the stairs to our flat. That would have been no small saving, as she had suffered from osteomyelitis as a young woman and her legs always gave her trouble.

But, instead of using the money, she banked it and only ever spent the interest. Many years later, when mother died, Wilma and I each inherited £200. My grandmother's £400 was divided between us.

Mother was a doer. She spent all her time doing, almost as though she was filling every minute in order to have no time left for feeling. Never do I remember her putting her arms around me and telling me she loved me. Dad was a quiet and sweet-natured man. I think in all my life I cannot remember him criticising anyone at all, including my mother.

I want to share these years, not because I have a need to vent my spleen, I don't, but because so many others have gone through similar circumstances, feeling they are different and carrying their burdens and hurts alone. I look back now and think of the many good attributes my mother had, but feel sad that she was brought up with harshness and criticism, which left her embittered and depressed. Her legacy to her daughters was teenage years spent in an atmosphere not dissimilar to that which had caused her own problems. Satan must be heartened when he creates and sustains such a cycle. Mother was a Christian and had access to the means of breaking the cycle, but she never did.

The hurt Mother experienced in her younger years was locked up inside her and never talked about, the key to open her past having been thrown away. Someone has said, 'To trust, to open ourselves to emotional communication with other people is to run the risk of being hurt. If we are hurt once, we can do one of two things. We can build a thick protective shell, or scar tissue to prevent being hurt again, live like an oyster, and not be hurt. Or we can turn the other cheek, remain vulnerable and go on living creatively.' All the past hurts she had received were hidden behind a thick protective wall. She could not accept herself for who she was. Because she had not felt loved as a child she had great difficulty expressing love. Had she been able to accept herself unconditionally she would have been released to accept others unconditionally too.

Kay Arthur, speaker and author, writes about this in her book *Teach Me to Live*. Kay believes that the only key that will fit the lock is love, not another being's love, although that plays a part, but rather a right love of self, a proper godly self-esteem. 'It is in knowing Jesus. I must gaze deeply into that Fountain of Living Water until I catch an image of what I am to him and what I am in him ... I will realise that I am unique, one of a kind, foreknown by him and marked out beforehand to become conformed to his image.' Sadly, my mother never knew this and so lived a defeated Christian life. How different it could have been had she released all her hurt to the One who longed to set her free from herself and from her past. To those of us who are struggling with a low self-esteem, the Lord offers to touch the deep recesses of our hearts and reveal our beauty even to ourselves, the beauty of those who are chosen to be the bride of Christ.

My childhood bore fruit in my life too: times of depression, an overwhelming need to feel wanted and an unChristian poor opinion of myself. But God worked in my soul. Before my teenage years were over I determined that should I ever have children they would know I loved them. They would know, not only because I cared for them and cleaned for them, but because I held them close and told them so.

Whatever my genetic inheritance from my mother, I know my father's legacy within me is my voice. Since my very earliest days I have loved singing, as has my sister Wilma. Our parents had a piano, which, along with a tiled close, was the hallmark of the Glasgow toff! Music was part of our lives. Dad wanted to teach me to play the bagpipes but I studied piano instead.

A lady who lived three up in a Springburn tenement building gave me lessons. She had very bad eyesight and could not clean her windows. I remember trying to help her by doing them for her. Cleaning the outsides meant sitting on the windowsill, three up, stretching as far as I could without falling to the ground below. The Lord, who laid it on my heart to help, cared for me.

I was privileged to be in the Scottish Co-operative Junior Singers led by Miss Agnes Duncan. The choir later became the Scottish Junior singers. The highlight of the year was our annual concert. This was held in St Andrew's Hall in Glasgow and Sir Hugh Roberton of the Orpheus Choir conducted us. My sister was also gifted with a voice and her song ministry has been used throughout central Scotland.

Singing was also the area in which I was able to serve my Lord. I believe he gave me not just a singing voice, but a singing ministry. And I thank him for it. Every Sunday school had its soiree and Bible classes their socials. Such occasions don't exist today. Children and adults alike did their party pieces, and singers and musicians were invited along to perform. I went all over Glasgow singing and could have engagements two or three times in a week. There was a wholesomeness in these evenings and a great deal of laughter and fun. Thinking back, I realise that my evenings were perhaps rather overfull for a teenager still at school. But home became increasingly unpleasant and my parents' relationship ever more strained. The life I led allowed me to be young.

When I was fourteen I started attending the SCYR, Scottish Christian Youth Rallies. These were founded by a Glasgow man, William McKinley. He was a man before his time, recognising that young people were open to the gospel and would respond to its challenge. Furthermore, he knew that new Christians would grow and flourish if given a place in which to mature. The SCYR took the Lyric Theatre in Glasgow's Sauchiehall Street for a month at a time and arranged gospel meetings every evening of the month. Men like Myrrdin Lewis, Stan Ford the boxer, Red Harpur, Alan Redpath – real men of God – came to speak to packed audiences and many were brought into a new and living relationship with the Lord.

The SCYR ran Converts' Classes on Wednesday nights in the Christian Institute in Bothwell Street. I went every week. We had a time of singing, which was followed by a speaker. Many who found Christ at the rallies and who were nurtured in the Converts' Classes are now ministers and leaders in churches around the world. There is a saying that 'you can count how many seeds are in an apple, but you cannot count how many apples are in a seed'. Seeds were planted in those days which have borne much fruit for the kingdom of God all round the world. And, as a result of meeting regularly through SCYR, many young people met their life partners and countless marriages and homes were established on biblical principles.

Predictably, I was a member of the SCYR choir, which held its weekly practice on Wednesdays after the Converts' Class. The choirmaster lived in Balornock and, if our practice ran late or we were out on deputation, he would get a taxi and drop me off in Springburn on his way home. Nothing seemed to be a trouble to these men of God and I ask myself where their likes are today. I think the answer is that they are kept from spending their free time in the Lord's service because business and professional demands are made on them that reduce their non-working hours to a minimum. Is this a tactic of the devil to stunt the growth of the next generation of believers? I fear it may well be.

Fridays found us back in the Christian Institute, this time for a meeting for prayer. Although my prayer life since then has been chequered, I look back on those Friday evenings and know that it was there that the foundation was laid for whatever service I have been able to offer to the Lord.

Central Scotland has always been the Bible Belt of the country. And that brought with it many privileges. One of them was a Sunday evening commitment as soloist at an open-air service held on the corner of Glasgow's Rose Street and Sauchiehall Street. Anything up to 200 people gathered to hear the gospel. A van, equipped with a public address system, was used. I usually sang to draw the crowds, and a hymn sung to the tune of the Londonderry Air was a popular choice. One evening, a man was breaking into a nearby office. When he heard the tune he joined the crowd at the open-air meeting where he heard the gospel and was saved. That kind of open-air witness seems to be a thing of the past. What a pity.

Accepting invitations to sing sometimes meant committing myself to quite a lot of travelling. As I earned £1 a week and gave my mother 16/- (80p) of it, money was in short supply. There were many times when I had to walk home because I was too shy to give an honest answer to, 'Do you have any expenses?' I am sure my singing was not blessed on those occasions because my thoughts were not at all spiritual as I walked home with sore feet and a sorer heart. It was thoughtlessness that prevented the question being avoided and expenses being given, but God used it in the long run to teach me that my singing was not to be for personal gain, but for his glory.

Despite all my distractions I came third in my third-year examinations at school. I was a plodder and this result came as a great surprise. I remember going home from school one day with the exciting news that my mother was invited to call at the school, Albert Secondary, to discuss my future with the headmaster. There was little discussion. Father did not enjoy good health and Mother had decided that I should leave school and find a job. They needed the extra income. Mr McRoberts, my headmaster, explained that he thought I might be able to go on to university. But Mother's mind was made up. I started work aged fifteen years in a lawyer's office in the centre of Glasgow, answering the telephone and making the tea. A few months later, I sat both the Railway and the Civil Service Examinations. Passing them both, I opted for the Civil Service and it was within that vast organisation that I worked until I was married.

Peter McFarlane's first recollection of seeing me was when I sang in the Tent Hall in Glasgow. That great Mission Hall was established as a result of one of D. L. Moody's Missions. It stood proudly in the centre of Glasgow and each Saturday evening it was packed with men, women and young folk from all around. The preaching was an inspiration. And the free breakfasts it provided were a blessing to many poor people who knew they would find compassion and a meal in the Tent Hall. The church was not just a religious and social club, meeting the needs of its members, rather it reached out to hurting humanity and helped people where they hurt most.

When I was fifteen years old, I met Peter on a Bible class bus run. I don't suppose it occurred to me that one day we would marry but, in those days, when you were going out with a boy you did not look around for an alternative. Peter was eighteen and a signwriter. He was brought up in the Christian Brethren and, like me, had been converted at the age of eleven. Peter did not join in my SCYR activities, preferring, on Wednesdays and Fridays, to play billiards in a hall nearby. He was, however, a fine pianist and he became my accompanist. Invitations for me to sing at soirees and socials began to include Peter, who was asked to play the piano accordion as well as accompany my singing. We were quite conscious that we were beginning to engage in a joint ministry.

Peter and Dad got on famously. But my mother and Peter did not get on at all. It was a difficult time for the family. Mum was in a deep depression and a rift between my parents, which had always been there, was widening. There was no question of either leaving. That alternative was borne of an affluence that did not exist until the sixties. In those days couples stuck it out, and often survived the crisis to produce a stronger marriage at the end of the day. In my parents' case they just stuck it out.

Mother's depression and Peter's mischievous nature did not blend well, while for Dad I think my boyfriend provided some light relief. And a mischief he most certainly was! David went with Peter to the Police Christian Fellowship. Bobby, who was a quiet fellow, also went. To leave the building after the meeting they had to pass a huge dinner gong. One evening, as they prepared to go, Peter and David removed the gong's striker and stuck it in Bobby's coat pocket. Bobby didn't notice, but the man at the door did. The guilty pair hid their merriment as Bobby carried the can for their nonsense. All men then wore coats and hats which they hung on rows of pegs during church services. Each man's hat was hooked above his coat. Given the opportunity, Peter and his pal would rearrange the hats, causing no end of confusion after the benediction had been pronounced. Such was my eighteen-year-old boyfriend!

A lack of money determined how young folk spent their courting days. If we felt wealthy and the weather was bad we went to the pictures to get out of the rain. My parents did not disapprove of the cinema at all. In fact, for a rare treat when we were girls, Mum took Wilma and I to see a film after school. I remember going to Snow White and others. Some people from Peter's more narrow background were less approving of our activities. More often, though, we went for a walk. Peter's sister Freda and her husband Jimmy were very good to us. We used to go to their house a lot where the four of us played board games: snakes and ladders, draughts, ludo and the like. We had a lot of fun together. Peter was always good company.

The time came for Peter to be conscripted into the Forces. I prayed that he would not get in, and in so doing realised how much I wanted him to stay. During his medical, it was discovered that he had a perforated eardrum and he was turned down on medical grounds. I had promised the Lord that if he kept Peter out of the forces we would serve him together. That is just what happened. Peter played for me and I sang. We did that throughout the whole of central Scotland for years, sometimes three or four times a week.

I was an avid reader. Books like *Mark of the Beast* and Isobel Kuhn's autobiography made a big impression on me. When I was seventeen I had a tonsillectomy and was quite ill for a time. We had a hole-in-the-wall bed and I lay in it reading a book entitled *In the Twinkling of an Eye*. Mother was out and Dad was working.

When it grew dark my imagination ran away with me. I began thinking that the Lord had come back to take his own people to heaven and that I had been left behind. Having given my heart to the Lord when I was eleven, had he come back he would have taken me with him, but my assurance wavered in the twilight.

My study of the Bible set me thinking about baptism. I don't think that the Foundry Boys practised baptism at all. So far as I remember, infants were dedicated rather than baptised. After much thought and prayer I asked for believer's baptism and was baptised in Abingdon Gospel Hall in Partick. A short time later I joined Springburn Gospel Hall near my home. Mother, I think, longed to go with me but would not. Years later she told me that she wished she had joined the Brethren when I did. Perhaps if she had we might have grown closer.

By that time it was clear that my relationship with Peter was serious but Mother's authority waned not a bit. 'I might not see what you are up to,' she would remind me as I left the house, 'but remember, "Thou God seest me"' (Gen. 16:13, AV). That kind of influence came through to me and I thank God for it. I think it helped prevent me, as a young person, getting involved in things that were unhelpful and unhealthy. The fact that God was watching me was always at the back of my mind, not in an oppressive way; it was something of a comfort.

Mother's rules were rigid. I was allowed out until 10 o'clock and not a minute beyond it. If I arrived home late I would find the house door locked. That presented something of a dilemma. I would hang about the door for a while hopefully, but that never opened it. Then, not knowing what else to do, I would take myself downstairs to the close where I waited for what I thought was a reasonable time before going back up and trying the door again. Sometimes I found it open and slunk in to face the music. On other occasions my mother was less yielding and I had to take myself down to the close once more for another period of penance before climbing wearily up again to try the door. If I am totally honest, one of the reasons I wanted to marry young was in order to be free of my restrictions. The other was that I loved Peter!

3

Life on the learning curve

Does the road wind uphill all the way?
Yes, to the very end.
Will the day's journey take the whole long day?
From morn to night, my friend.
(Christina Georgina Rossetti)

Peter and I were engaged when I was nineteen. He trained as a signwriter under Mr Andrew Mars, a heraldic artist, and worked with him and one other young man. They did fine work, and had the contract to do the coachwork signwriting for some big companies including Scottish Motor Transport. I worked in the Income Tax Office, earning £3 18/6 (£3.92½p) a week. From that I gave my mother £2 for my keep. I also had a Saturday job in one of Springburn's departmental stores for 10/- (50p). Peter did odd jobs at night as well as working for Mr Mars. We were saving for our wedding.

Just like my mother, I locked my hurts away. My self-esteem was almost nil. When Peter and I went to parties I sat alone thinking how much prettier all the other girls were and how much better dressed they were. I tortured myself with the thought that Peter would find them more attractive than me. Many of these nights found me withdrawing into myself and holding a pity party at which I was the only guest!

It was years later I discovered that self-pity is really the enthronement of self. Nothing obliterates God from our minds as effectively as placing ourselves on his throne. And such terrible conceit renders us temporarily useless to him.

A friend of ours, David Anderson, who was a partner in a property-letting firm, found us our first house in Raeberry Street, in the Maryhill district of Glasgow. It was in a terrible state. But we worked at it and made it as comfortable as we could. Mother gave us £50 for a deposit on a three-piece suite and with the dowry of £100 I was given when I left the Income Tax Office we bought a piano. We were halfway to being toffs! A friend's sister made the dresses and we booked the Burlington Hotel for both the wedding and reception. Not many of our friends had cars and to have been married in a Gospel Hall and then travelled to the hotel for our reception would have added to their expenses quite a bit. The Burlington had a little chapel and it was in it that we were to be married.

Some weeks before our wedding Peter and I were invited to friends for supper after a singing engagement. It was a beautiful meal. 'That's how I want you to be able to spread a table', Peter told me, as we walked home afterwards. Panic rose within me. I couldn't cook! Money had always been so tight that there was none extra for the trial and errors that are the inevitable results of early cooking and baking. That, coupled with my mother's critical attitude to my efforts at anything, left me totally ill-equipped to run a home. I can't do it, I thought over and over again as I wept myself to sleep on the nights that followed.

As the wedding drew closer, things at home became more and more difficult. The stress of my leaving seemed to affect my mother badly. As she was fifty-five years old by then you would have thought the time had come for her to see me go quite happily. On the night before our wedding Wilma was out and I knelt beside the bed I was about to share with her for the last time. 'Lord,' I prayed, 'please make me a good wife.' I was full of uncertainty and apprehension about the future. I knew I had no real idea what being a wife was about, or the responsibility it would bring. At the same time I was excited. No longer would I have to be in by 10pm! And I had, I think, the feeling a child must have when she knows she's going to be given a new toy – a doll's house.

On 5th February, 1955, Jessie Robertson and Peter McFarlane were married. At last we were man and wife. Moving into our little house we made light of its disadvantages. Peter was patient with my domestic ineptitude. Handkerchiefs did not, he told me, need to be starched! And I discovered for myself that a whole pound of barley was rather too much for one pan of soup. The barley had a memorable way of showing me that was the case. Knowing it did a carpet square good to be turned, I turned mine every week! This was a major operation, involving as it did the removal of all our furniture from the room. Having found a job in the local Department of Social Services office, I tried to do all this before I went to work in the morning. What I looked like when I arrived in the office on my carpet turning days I would rather not try to imagine.

God knew my shortcomings and needs and provided for them. Some years before, when I sang at their church, we had made friends with an elderly couple. Now we found ourselves living across the road from them. They were mentors to us in so many ways, and how much I owe to Aunt May, as I called her, in regard to my housekeeping skills. She was a great cook and a lovely baker. Every Friday night I went over to her flat to watch her cook and bake. Her practical example and many tips have stood me in good stead ever since. Nine months after we were married my parents celebrated their twenty-fifth wedding anniversary. They, along with twenty-one others, were invited to our little home and I cooked and presented a meal for all twenty-five! At the time its success was probably seen as just a stroke of good fortune. But God used that occasion to encourage me in Christian hospitality and since then it has been our joy to open our home and welcome people from all over the world.

I write this now, fifty-six years on, and would like to encourage those of you who may be in the early years of your marriage. The Bible is the finest textbook from which we as Christian women learn our responsibility to our homes. We are 'to love [our] husbands, love [our] children, to be sensible, pure, workers at home, kind, being subject to [our] own husbands, so that the word of God will not be dishonoured' (Titus 2:4-5, NASB).

The home was the first organization to be founded by God. The examples of the women in the Bible with whom God was pleased indicate that the home was their main sphere of service for God (Sarah, Jochabed and Hannah). Proverbs 31 shows us what God wants a wife to be, and our responsibility to our home is a God-given one. In verse 30 the wording indicates that the motivation for being an efficient wife, homemaker and mother is fear of the Lord.

Have you ever noticed that the tenor of your home depends a lot on how you feel each day? Our attitude can pretty well determine how things will go for each member of our family. I look back and remember times when this was so true. If I was depressed and uptight, that sent signals down through the family and it was not a 'good day'. The responsibility of the happiness of the home often falls on us as mothers. Someone has said, 'men build houses, women make homes'. A happy Christian home is a place centred on people, not things, where God is the centre and source of everything that happens in that home. As wives and mothers we have a tremendous responsibility, not only to our families, but to the Lord to make a good job of what he has given us to do. Looking back over the years, I thank God for his grace and mercy which has enabled me to fulfil and enjoy, to the best of my abilities, my role as wife and mother.

In the first year of our marriage God saw fit to use our ministry among young people. He had an amazing way of introducing us to contemporaries who had come from the same kind of background as ourselves. There was Hugh and Anne. A firm Peter did some work for employed Hugh, a heavy drinker. Peter got alongside him, inviting him to go to a meeting at which the evangelist, Peter Brandon, was speaking. Hugh went and found the Lord. We still meet people today, over fifty years later, who remember being in our home at that time.

About a year after we were married, Peter came home from work one night with some news. Mr Mars, his employer, was in his seventies, and the other young man who worked with Peter had taken a realistic look at their situation and decided to branch out on his own. 'I'll have to do the same, I suppose,' Peter concluded. And so he did. We were young and did not realise the problems and pitfalls involved in Peter working for himself. Had we done so we might not have gone into it so lightly, especially as I became pregnant with our first child at about that time. Things started well, though, with Peter taking over some of the big contracts which Mr Mars' firm had done previously.

Three months later, major problems arose. I became ill with toxemia and was taken to hospital. That very same day Peter developed appendicitis and needed surgery. As neither of us was able to work we had no money coming in. I had often sung,

> I trust in God wherever I may be
> Upon the land or on the rolling sea.
> For come what may, from day to day,
> My Heavenly Father watches over me.

I had sung those words and they had moved my spirit. But I had never really proved their reality in my life. I had to do so now. For the remaining four months of my pregnancy I was confined to bed. My mother was a great help in keeping the house running. It was at times like that I really appreciated her 'doing' nature. And friends appeared unexpectedly, just when we most needed them. God did indeed watch over us. Spiritually we were on a rollercoaster. We passed through some dark days when it seemed that our prayers rose no higher than the ceiling. Then there were others when we were so conscious of God's presence and saw it in very many practical ways.

One precious memory concerns Jean Macmillan. Jean had been my boss in the hardware department of the store in Springburn in which I worked each Saturday. She had such a sweet spirit and was a real friend over these difficult months. Peter and I were just home from hospital when Jean came to visit us. As she left that evening she slipped something under my pillow. Can you imagine our amazement when Peter and I discovered that she had given us her week's pay packet, unopened? Her act of compassion overwhelmed us both and assured us again of God's provision.

Times like these were a challenge to me because my walk with God was not always as it should have been. In those early-married years especially, it was a very public thing. Certainly I adored and worshipped God when I sang songs of praise to him, but my private devotional life was sometimes non-existent in any structured kind of way. Yet God blessed my singing ministry. In my heart of hearts I longed to walk more closely with my Saviour, and I think it was this that God blessed. I tried to be obedient.

I have often since pondered on the words God spoke through the psalmist, 'I will instruct you and teach you in the way you should go; I will counsel you and watch over you. Do not be like the horse or the mule, which have no understanding but must be controlled by bit and bridle or they will not come to you' (Ps. 32:8-9). Had I studied and believed God's Word I could have shed so many of my doubts and fears. I would have been able to rest on his precious promises.

> 'I know the plans I have for you,' declares the LORD, 'plans to prosper you and not to harm you, plans to give you hope and a future. Then you will call upon me and come and pray to me, and I will listen to you. You will seek me and find me when you seek me with all your heart. I will be found by you,' declares the LORD, 'and will bring you back from captivity' (Jer. 29:11-14).

But instead of seeking him diligently, he had to control me with bit and bridle to make me follow him. And the bits and the bridles which he used were problems and ill health such as I experienced over these months of confinement. God will go to miracle lengths to make us pay attention.

It is a sad fact that when things are going well for us we tend to ignore God and do our own thing. Often it is only when he leads us through suffering and pain that we cry out to him for help. C. S. Lewis, in his book *The Problem of Pain*, describes suffering as 'God's megaphone'. He says, 'God whispers to us in our pleasures, speaks in our conscience, but God shouts in our pains'. What a slow learner I was in this school. When God shouted I was obedient and sought the Lord for a while ... until the crisis was over. Then I headed off on my own again. God often allowed me to suffer the consequences of my disobedience.

Dee and Paul Goodwin, who spoke many years later at a Prayer Chain Conference, told of their experience of going down the road of disobedience. Dee was convinced that God was leading them to move home, but Paul was adamant that they should stay where they were. They decided to make some improvements to their central heating system. While working on the gas radiators the workmen discovered they had forgotten the caps to cap the pipes, and further forgot to turn off the gas when they went to collect them! The gas built up inside the empty house until the inevitable happened, the building exploded.

All that remained of their furniture was the piano. Dee and Paul collected it and were driving away from the wreck of their former home when Paul burst out laughing. 'What is there to laugh about?' his wife asked. 'Well,' said Paul, 'I have just had a picture of God leaning over the balustrade of heaven with a megaphone in his hand, asking if I can hear him now!'

It is my experience that, because God's purpose is to make us Christlike, he has to destroy the dross in our lives and when he has dealt with one area, e.g. our temper or our pride, and we are obedient to what he asks of us, he then moves on to another, using whatever means it takes to change us. Obedience is the outward expression of our love for God, and the reward of obedience and love is that He will reveal himself to us. 'The one who obeys me is the one who loves me; and because he loves me, my Father will love him; and I will too, and I will reveal myself to him' (John 14:21 TLB).

If we have an obedience problem, we have a love problem, in many ways obedience is our moment of truth. What we do will reveal what we believe about

God and determine whether we will experience his mighty work in us and through us. It will also determine whether we will come to know him more intimately. I haven't been able to find who said, 'All God's revelations are sealed until they are opened by the key of obedience. The tiniest fragment of obedience and heaven opens and the profound truths of God are ours. God will never reveal more truth about Himself until we have obeyed what we already know.' But I believe it. **But God** will not move us on if we do not obey him! For most of us obedience is to what we see to be a need, but the Lord's obedience was to the will of his Father. How did he know his Father's will? He prayed.

I find it helpful to compare this process of sanctification to the following picture. In my mind I see myself as a living house that God comes to rebuild. At first I understand what he is doing: he is getting the drains right, stopping the leaks in the roof and other things that I can see need done.

But then he starts knocking the house about in a way that really hurts, and that doesn't seem to make sense. What on earth is he up to? The explanation is that he is building quite a different house – throwing out a new wing here, putting on an extra floor there, running up towers, making courtyards, changes I could not have imagined possible. I thought I was going to be made into a decent little cottage but instead God is building a palace, a palace in which he will live!

Oswald Chambers says, 'God's order has to work up to a crisis in our lives because we will not heed the gentler way. He brings us to the place where he asks us to be our utmost for him and we begin to debate; then he produces a providential crisis where we have to decide for or against, and from that point on the "Great Divide" begins.'

Those early years of marriage, walking an unknown path, were exciting and scary. I am glad the unknown path was all marked out in the blueprint of my life before I was even a twinkle in my father's eye. '[Y]our eyes saw my unformed body. All the days ordained for me were written in your book before one of them came to be' (Ps. 139:16).

I love this poem. Its author is unknown.

Child of my love, fear not the unknown morrow.
Dread not the new demand life makes of thee;
Your ignorance shall hold no cause for sorrow,
For what you do not know is known to me.

You cannot see today the hidden meaning
Of my command, but you the light shall gain
Walk on in faith, upon my promise leaning,
And as you go, all shall be made plain.

One step you see: then go forward boldly;
One step is far enough for faith to see.
Take that, and your next duty shall be told thee,
For step by step your God is leading thee.

Stand not in fear your adversaries counting:
Dare every peril save to disobey.
You shall march on, each obstacle surmounting,
For I, the Strong, shall open up the way.

Therefore go gladly to the task assigned you,
Having my promise; needing nothing more
Than just to know where e'er the future find you,
In all your journeying – I GO BEFORE.

Isaiah said that the Lord spoke to him with a strong hand. That strong hand was evidenced in the pressure of circumstances. There is nothing that touches our lives, but it is God speaking. So often we only discern the circumstances, but not his hand on our lives. How I wish I had understood these great truths more as a young wife facing motherhood with all the joys, sorrows and challenges that it would bring. Surely God's strong hand is nowhere felt more keenly than in the rearing of a family.

All through history the Lord has used families as the place of both blessing and proving. The original earthly family started with problems. The first son ever born, Cain, murdered the first brother ever born, Abel, in a jealous fit. In one day Adam and Eve lost their only two sons because Cain instantly became a fugitive as punishment for Abel's murder.

As a teen, Joseph was taken and sold into slavery by his brothers. He went through thirteen years of severe testing before he was promoted to be second in command in Egypt. It was still another nine years before he was reunited with his family. Joseph was separated from his family for twenty-two years. He was a slave and a prisoner before he became Prime Minister. God uses our families to hone, mature and bring us often to our knees. But they can also be a real blessing and bring us much joy as they mature into responsible adults. '[C]hildren are an heritage from the LORD, and the fruit of the womb is his reward. As arrows are in the hand of a mighty man, so are children of the youth. Happy is the man that hath his quiver full of them, they shall not be ashamed, but they shall speak with the enemies in the gate' (Ps. 27:3-5, KJV).

In a 'Decision' magazine some years ago, Dr Billy Graham stated that a survey was taken to determine the strongest factor in children's character development. The surprising conclusion was that more than anything else, the overall atmosphere of the home, particularly the attitude of the mother, helped to form their characters.

The Bible gives several illustrations of God-fearing mothers dedicating their children to the Lord and praying for them, women such as Hannah, mother of Samuel, who became one of Israel's greatest prophets. Hannah is a woman one can relate to. She lived in dark days nationally, spiritually and personally. Spiritually the nation was in darkness. We read in 1 Samuel 3:1 that 'And the word of the LORD was rare in those days; there was no frequent vision' (ESV).

Personally the days were dark. Hannah had a deep personal sorrow, she had no children. The one bright light on the horizon was that her husband Elkanah loved her. But Elkanaha's second wife Peninah made her life a misery and she gave Hannah a hard time. We get an insight into Hannah's feelings in 1 Samuel 1. Peninah so provoked her that she did not eat, she wept bitterly and was greatly distressed.

Hannah was afflicted and oppressed in her spirit, but she went to the One she knew who understood her sorrow, and she prayed. Her prayer was born out of suffering and heartbreak. Have you ever been there? Some call it 'wits-end-corner'. I've been there, and oh, how comforting to go to One who is never taken by surprise by the traumas we pass through. Hannah knew her God!

Personal trials can be used to refine our faith (1 Pet. 1:5-7). They can bring us to maturity (James 1:2-4). Perseverance through trial produces character (Rom. 5:3-5). We learn discipline that produces a harvest of righteousness and peace (Heb. 12:7-9).

When Hannah prayed, she did not ask something for herself. She made a vow that if God would give her a son, she would give him back to him. When she prayed that prayer, I'm quite sure she had no idea just how it would be answered. Hannah made a vow to the Lord that if he gave her a son, a razor would not come on his head. He would be a Nazarite, which means that he would be bound by a vow of consecration to God's service. Hannah did not pray something for her son that she had not lived by herself. She kept her vow to God.

Before our four children were born, my husband and I gave them to the Lord, and our prayer was that they would become men and women of God for their generation. This is still our prayer, whatever paths they have chosen.

We are not told much more about Hannah, other than God opened her womb and she had another three sons and two daughters. Because of a praying honourable mother, and God's purposes for his life, Samuel grew both in favour with God and man, and yet 1 Samuel 3:7 tells us, 'Now Samuel did not yet know the LORD, nor had the word of the LORD yet been revealed to him' (NASB). God's hand was on his life in the midst of a wicked situation (1 Sam. 2:12-26).

We read in 1 Samuel. 3:1 that '[I]n those days the word of the LORD was rare; there were not many visions.' The nation was in darkness. Then something happened. 'And Samuel grew, and the LORD was with him and he let none of his words fall to the ground. And all Israel from Dan to Beersheba knew that Samuel was established as a prophet of the LORD. And the LORD appeared again at Shiloh, for the LORD revealed himself to Samuel at Shiloh by the word of the LORD' (1 Sam. 3:19-21, ESV). Because of an honorable praying mother and an obedient child, the nation of Israel was blessed.

We have a responsibility to teach our children. 'These words, which I am commanding you today, shall be on your heart. You shall teach them diligently to your sons and shall talk of them when you sit in your house and when you walk by the way and when you lie down and when you rise up' (Deut. 6:6-7, NASB).

Sadly our children do not always follow what they have been taught. The saying, 'God doesn't have any grandchildren', expresses that our children cannot come to the Lord on *our* faith, they must exercise their own faith in Jesus Christ. A time comes when they make their own decisions in life and they choose to go their own way. This keeps us on our knees, and causes us to be persistent in prayer for the prodigals.

It is by authority from the Lord that the father should be the one to be responsible for the spiritual well-being of the family. But if he is not available, then the responsibility devolves to the mother. I have great admiration for women who, through various circumstances, are left to bring up their children alone, and there are many today in these circumstances. They not only have to be a mother, but also a breadwinner.

This demands great strength of character. For those who have been widowed, God has promised to be a '[f]ather of the fatherless and protector of widows' (Ps. 68:5, ESV).

In the New Testament, God gives the examples of Lois and Eunice, who passed on their knowledge and faith to Timothy. There is no mention of his father (2 Tim. 1:5). John Mark, who wrote the Gospel of Mark and travelled with the Apostle Paul, grew up under the influence of a godly mother (Acts 12:12).

What a responsibility it is to be given the wonderful opportunity to be 'missionaries' in our own homes! We may never cross the seas to Africa or Asia, but we could be raising a David Livingstone, a Mary Slessor, a Corrie ten Boom, a Billy Graham, a man or woman of God who could be used to bring many to Christ. Not too much is known about many of the godly mothers who raised such children. But the influence they had on their families is evident in the impact these men and women have made for God in their generations.

This should be an encouragement to those of us who have children. We only get one 'bite at the apple', as time goes past so quickly, and they are gone from the nest. May I also encourage those of you who do not have children? To some this may be a real sorrow, but you can be a big influence in the lives of your nieces, nephews and in the children of your friends. I can think of many women over the years who did not have the joy of children of their own but they made an impact on my life spiritually as they encouraged me and prayed for me. My sister Wilma and I often remark that where God has taken us in our Christian witness for him is the result of people praying for us.

How wonderful it has been for me during the compiling of this book to look back and see how God has gone before me, preparing situations and people (vital links) to be part of his plan for my life. Shona was born just before Christmas 1957. She was fine, a perfect healthy baby. I nearly died at her birth. So ill was I that I lost my sight for two days following delivery. The first thing I remember was the smell of hyacinths. Freda, my sister-in-law, had been to visit and had brought the flowers with her.

I was one of only two patients in the ward. The other was a communist, and how she harangued the sister as she put up the Christmas tree. She tore the Health Service apart until the sister could take it no longer. 'The Health Service will save lives,' she told the belligerent young woman. 'And it was only because of the Health Service we could call in a specialist three times when he was needed for Mrs McFarlane, without worrying about whether or not she could afford it. And if we hadn't been able to do that, she would have died.' I knew I had been ill. Only then did I realise how seriously.

Shona was a lovely baby, a real gift from God. Having decided long before I was married that if I had children I would love in words as well as actions, I set about doing just that. How often Shona had the words 'I love you' whispered in her warm little ears. When she was just six months old we moved from our first flat in Maryhill to a larger one in Hyndland. Trailing a pram up three flights of stairs was too much for me in my weakened state.

We moved our membership to Abingdon Hall in the West End, and in that large fellowship we found godly men and women who were a real help to us as we tried to live our Christian lives. Our new flat became a haven for many who were struggling. Peter and I did not set ourselves up as counsellors, it was rather the opposite. God used us in all our weakness to reach out to others, many of whom we could readily identify with. How privileged we were to have these opportunities of service.

As soon as I became pregnant for the second time my doctor took me under her wing and cared for me like Dresden china! When Graham was born in June 1959, the labour-room staff must have thought I was mad, so excited was I at really participating in his birth. Perhaps they understood a little better when the doctor explained that I had been unconscious when our first child was born. My busy life became even busier, revolving round washing, cooking and all the other duties of a wife and mother. Peter had more than just fatherly commitments; he had his business to run, and enjoyed involvement in our local church, prison work and with Christian businessmen.

My Christian life became routine, with a form of godliness but little power. Prayer and Bible study were fit in only when I had time. I received little out of my reading of God's Word, and my prayers were determined by my needs. If I needed something, I went to God with my shopping list. Looking back, I am amazed how God preserved me through these vulnerable times of struggling on in my own strength.

Stuart Briscoe says that for many of us the Christian life is like an old iron bedstead, firm at both ends, but sagging in the middle. I was just like that. I knew I was saved. I knew I was going to heaven. But the bit in-between was sagging and sad.

Faithless though we often were, God guarded our footsteps. I look back and see that on many occasions when Peter and I could have made wrong decisions, God blocked the way. Opportunities for involvement in business, which might have provided more money but which would have got in the way of God's service, he took from us. Our disappointments were his appointments! I believe only eternity will reveal how our heavenly Father's goodness and mercy followed all the days of our lives. 'He has cared for us again and again here in the wilderness, just as a father cares for his child' (Deut. 1:31 TLB). 'For this great God is our God for ever and ever. He will be our guide until we die' (Ps. 48:14, TLB).

When Graham was only months old he became suddenly very ill. For a week he screamed when he was touched, and most of the time when he was lying on his own. I couldn't change him or dress him without causing my little baby such great distress. Towards the end of the week he was quiet. I decided to change him before the visitors we were expecting arrived. On taking off his tiny clothes I discovered that his little chest was terribly swollen and red as a robin redbreast. With an upstairs neighbour we rushed him by taxi to Yorkhill Hospital where he was admitted with what was thought to be osteomyelitis.

Investigations discovered an abscess on his breast bone. Graham was in hospital for a week having the abscess drained. It was a painful experience for our dear little son, and a traumatic time for us. My mother's practical skills were a tremendous help at that time. She was such a worker, and always there when I needed her.

Busyness continued to keep me from a regular quiet time. Although I am sorry about that and know it was something I missed very much, I constantly talked to the Lord and I was always in an attitude of repentance. I suppose that was one way in which my upbringing was positively used. Self-examination was second nature to me, borne of worrying if all the things that my mother said to me and of me were true. Yet if I have been of any use in the Lord's service it is due, in part I am sure, to his deliverance from my unhappy relationship with my mother and his use of it to me.

Those early experiences continued to dog my life, causing periods of deep depression. They were lonely times because I withdrew from Peter and I think he withdrew from me. I don't blame him for that as I occasionally treated him very badly, going for days without speaking to him. Peter didn't seem to be able to understand, but I don't think that men did in those days. How hard it must have been for him because I found comfort in the children while he was unable to help me. And how hurt he must sometimes have felt when I could be nice to people who came to the house and be unpleasant to him. In these dark days I was driven in desperation to my knees and to my Bible.

The book of Psalms was a treasure chest as I could relate to David and what he went through. He described exactly what I felt and I could use his words to cry out of my desperation to God. 'How long, O LORD? Will you forget me for ever? How long will you hide your face from me? How long must I wrestle with my thoughts and every day have sorrow in my heart? How long will my enemy triumph over me?' (Ps. 13:1-2).

This experience is sometimes described as 'the dark night of the soul', when I could no longer feel the presence of God, but sensed only loneliness, and even nothingness. Thomas Merton makes the claim that these night times of the senses increase in frequency as time goes on, that there is a sense in which they can be taken as signs of progress provided the prayer does not give up, but determines to respond to the challenge, refuses to view this hollowness as spiritual doom or punishment for sin, but rather sees it for what it really is: the opportunity for growth.

I regret that it took me so long to realize that in the midst of this 'dark night' I could have made a choice, rather than say with Jacob in Genesis 42:36: '[A]ll these things are against me' (KJV). I could have said with Paul in Romans 8:28: 'And we know that in all things God works for good of those who love him, who have been called according to his purpose.' Corrie Ten Boom has said, 'when a train goes through a tunnel the world gets dark. Do you jump off? No of course not, you sit still and trust the engineer to get you through.'

With the passing of each period of depression I slid into my old ways, talking to God as I busied myself being a wife, a mother and a gospel singer, but neglecting times of searching for him in his Word and pleading with him in prayer. Now I see my mistake. I was resting on the warm assurance that God knew the plans he had for me and that his plans were for good, not for ill. But I was neglecting to be obedient to his command in the same passage of Scripture. '"You will seek me and find me when you seek me with all your heart. I will be found by you," declares the LORD, "and will bring you back from captivity"' (Jer. 29:13-14). I was taking God for granted. And because I was making no real effort to seek for him I found myself from time to time in the captivity of depression. It was years later that I was released. I had many painful lessons to learn before then.

All of us experience hurt over and again in our lives. It may be financial or social loss, unemployment, rebellious children, an unfaithful partner, or something much less threatening. The important thing is not what hurts us but how we choose to deal with that hurt.

I like the rendering of Hebrews 12:11 in *The Message*. 'God is educating you; that's why you must never drop out. He's treating you as dear children. This trouble you're in isn't punishment; its training, the normal experience of children. Only irresponsible parents leave children to fend for themselves. Would you prefer an irresponsible God?' It's not what happens to us that matters, but how we respond.

We respect our parents for training rather than spoiling us, even though they only did what *seemed* best to them. But as God *knows* what is best for us, why don't we embrace his training? It is because discipline hurts, it is always against the grain. But discipline is never lost, it pays off handsomely in terms of our relationship with God and our effectiveness in this world. In all things and through all things God is working for our good. And against the power of God the whole array of Satan's forces is just a matchstick army.

So, what do you think? With God on our side like this how can we lose? If God didn't hesitate to put everything on the line for us, embracing our condition and exposing himself to the worst by sending his own Son, is there anything else he wouldn't gladly and freely do for us? And who would dare tangle with God by messing with one of God's chosen? Who would dare even to point a finger? The One who died for us – who was raised to life for us! – is in the presence of God at this very moment sticking up for us. Do you think anyone is going to be able to drive a wedge between us and Christ's love for us? There is no way!' (Rom. 8:31-34, MSG).

4

'Lord, make me real'

I falter where I firmly trod,
And falling with my weight of cares
Upon the great world's altar-stairs
That slope thro' darkness up to God.
(Alfred, Lord Tennyson)

Life was busy. We moved to Bishopbriggs in the north of Glasgow to a house that would be our home for many years. Twenty months after Graham was born, his little sister Karen arrived. My days were spent caring for Peter and the children, visiting my parents who had by then moved to East Kilbride, giving hospitality and fulfilling some singing engagements. It was after one such engagement that God used an old lady to open my eyes to the barrenness of my soul. I had just sung the words:

All my days and all my hours
All my will and all my powers
All the passion of my soul
Not a fragment but the whole
Shall be thine, O Lord.

She came up to me at the end of the singing. Shaking my hand and looking right into my eyes the old lady said, 'I can see that's real to you, dear.' If she had hit me over the face with a cold kipper I could not have been more taken aback. God was not that real to me. He did not have all my days and all my hours. I was a phoney, an absolute hypocrite. I was unreal. I wore my mask well and did all the right things. But deep in my heart there was emptiness.

What does it mean to be real? Bernard Levin, one of the greatest columnists of his generation, wrote in an article called *Life's Great Riddle and no Time to find its Meaning*, 'He feared that he might have wasted reality in the chase of a dream.'

One of the most moving beautiful books in the Bible is the story of Ruth and Naomi. Ruth is a wonderful example of someone who found reality and whose story shines through the pages of the Old Testament like a bright star in the night sky. Only two books in the Bible are named after women. Esther, who was a Jewess and married a Gentile, and Ruth, who was a Gentile and married a Jew, God used both these women in the preservation of his people at a time when the cause of truth was, in the eyes of men, unreal. But in reality, God's truth was marching on in triumph.

In the book of Ruth we are introduced to Naomi and Elimelech who lived in Bethlehem. Because a famine had ravished the land, they left and arrived in Moab, where there was full and plenty. But God had forbidden his people to have any contact with the Moabites or Ammonites (Deut. 23:3), and Elimelech grievously sinned in doing what he did. They were not long in the land of Moab when Elimelech died, and Naomi was left with her two sons, Mahlon and Chilion. They also sinned against God by marrying Moabite women. Mahlon married Ruth and Chilion married Orpah.

After some years, Mahlon and Chilion died and Ruth and Orpah were left, like Naomi, widows. When Elimelech and Naomi went to Moab they expected to enjoy a good life, but instead they suffered broken hearts and unfulfilled dreams. **BUT GOD**, how I love those two words. The 'buts' in Scripture are always worth noticing; they usually introduce a total contrast to what has gone before. God is saying that he has plans that allow things to come into the lives of men and women to refine, take away the dross and make us real. He brings us through the shadow, water and fire and *'brought us to a place of abundance'* (Ps. 66:12, emphasis added).

Ruth's background was one of idolatry, but she came to acknowledge her husband and her father and mother-in-law's God, and as she grew in her faith she learned that the God in whom she had put her trust was real and could provide food when there was no food, shelter when there was no shelter. He could give hope when there was no hope.

Eventually, Naomi learned that the famine in the land of Judah had ended and that while Naomi, Ruth and Orpah were starving in Moab, there was plenty of bread in Bethlehem. Naomi came to her senses and she decided to return home. It often takes tragedy to bring us to our senses, to wake us up to our spiritual condition. It is all too easy to become so established in our Christian routine that we lose our disciplines of prayer, reading God's Word and glorifying him in our lives. Losing our love and devotion to God can happen so subtly through busyness, discouragement and a host of other intrusions. Alan Redpath, once minister at Charlotte Chapel in Edinburgh, told how he had a plinth on his desk which said 'Beware of the barrenness of a busy life.' We can so easily be caught up with being 'busy, busy, busy' and think that we are doing God's will, but have we spent time in prayer asking God what he wants us to do? Jesus only did the things his Father told him to do. Prayer set the agenda for his choice of disciples in Luke 6:12-16. Prayer preceded his miracles in John 11:41-42. Prayer brought him encouragement at critical moments in his life. See Luke 9:28-31. So we need to guard against losing our disciplines of prayer and reading God's Word.

BUT GOD will not let us settle for second best. He wants reality in our lives and, as Oswald Chambers says in his book, *My Utmost for His Highest*, 'When we choose deliberately to obey him, then, with all his almighty power, he will tax the remotest star and the last grain of sand to assist us.'

So Naomi set out with her daughters-in-law. On the way Naomi wept and told them to go back to Moab, to their own people where they might find other husbands and new lives. The reality of finding God is seen in Ruth's life as she entreats Naomi not to ask her to go back or leave her. Ruth was prepared to go wherever Naomi went, for Naomi's people to be her people and Naomi's God to be her God. Naomi probably would have talked to Ruth and Orpah about the God of Israel and the wonderful signs and wonders he had performed in releasing his people from Egypt, not because they deserved it, but because he had chosen them to be his own people. I'm sure she prayed that God would open their hearts. Ruth responded because she saw reality in her mother-in-law's life.

Orpah only went so far with them and then in tears decided to return to Moab where she had grown up. Reality for Orpah was back in Moab with her pagan gods. Naomi and Ruth may well have thought that Orpah had changed, but she had not changed. It is possible that we may have been brought through difficult circumstances and great moving experiences, and yet there has not been a real change in our lives. Orpah heard through Naomi that God had visited Judah and there was full and plenty there, and so she set out to go there. Although she left Moab, however, her heart was still there and she decided to go back. Ruth made her decision to go with Naomi because for her there was nothing in Moab anymore.

Naomi and Ruth arrive in Bethlehem and the story goes on to see Ruth marry Boaz, who became her kinsman redeemer. She bore him a son named Obed, which means 'a servant', who through God's eternal purposes was a *'type'* of the supreme Servant, the Lord Jesus Christ. Obed brought great joy and consolation to Naomi in her old age. There is not much known about him other than he was the grandfather of King David. God's rich blessing was on Boaz and Ruth and her name became famous and was included in the genealogy of the Lord Jesus Christ (Matt. 1).

I love the wholesomeness of this lady, Ruth. It is so good to meet people who are 'wholesome', real people, with whom you can just be yourself, with no stress or strain. Dinah Maria Craik writes: 'Oh, the comfort, the inexpressible comfort, of feeling safe with a person; having neither to weigh thoughts nor measure words, but to pour them all out just as they are, chaff and grain together, knowing that a faithful hand will take and sift them, keep what is worth keeping, and with the breath of kindness, blow the rest away.' To me this is the evidence of a real friend, when one does not have to 'weigh words', or wonder if they have another agenda.

Do you, like me, struggle with the desire to be all that God wants us to be? I must confess that I am not always honest. When asked, 'How are you?' my standard reply is usually, 'I'm fine.' And what does FINE stand for? **F**eeling **I**nadequate and **N**eeding **E**ncouragement! Sometimes we are less than honest and this has an effect on our relationships. Our Christian love for each other should be sincere, genuine, honest, pure and unadulterated. This, Jesus said, would be how the world would know that we are his disciples, if we have love one for another.

The antithesis of reality is unreal, fake, false and counterfeit. When the Holy Spirit is shed abroad in our hearts, the first thing he does is to remove pretence and hypocrisy. This real love does not come from us, it comes from God and it is only there when the Holy Spirit has shed it abroad in our hearts. He reveals that God loved us not because we were loveable, but because it was his nature to do so, and he expects us to show the same love to others. 'Love as I have loved you.'

While I longed for reality and victory, my experience was of defeat. Alexander Whyte, in his book *Bible Characters*, wrote 'If you would move me with your preaching, or with your singing, or with your praying, first be moved yourself.' Hurrying home, I could not wait to be alone before the Lord. 'Lord,' I poured out my soul, 'Lord, make me real.'

Sometimes the simplest picture is the most vivid. So it is that the reality I sought is best described by Margery Williams in *The Velveteen Rabbit*. A new toy rabbit had arrived in the nursery and in speaking to the old rocking horse he discovers the secret of being real.

'What is real?' asked the rabbit one day when they were side by side by the nursery fire. 'Does it mean having things buzz inside you, a stick out handle?'

'Real isn't how you are made,' said the old rocking horse. 'It's a thing that happens to you when a child loves you for a long, long time, not just to play with, but really loves you. Then you become real.'

'Does it hurt?' asked the rabbit.

'Sometimes,' said the rocking horse, for he was always truthful. 'When you are real you don't mind being hurt.'

'Does it happen all at once? Like being wound up?' Rabbit asked, 'or bit by bit?'

'It doesn't happen all at once,' said the rocking horse. 'You become it, it takes a long time. That's why it doesn't happen to people who break easily or have sharp edges, or have to be carefully kept. Generally by the time you are real, most of your hair has been loved off. You are loose in the joints and very shabby. But these things don't matter at all because once you are real you can't be ugly except to those who don't understand.'

Bit by bit, through adversity and illness, God drew me towards the reality for which I prayed. In the midst of the busyness I began to make time to study his Word.

And I discovered that when we go 10 per cent of the way in God's direction he comes 90 per cent of the way in ours. As I read and studied Isaiah he lit up a verse with fluorescent lights! '"You are my servant"; I have chosen you' (Isa. 41:9). I had no doubt read it often, but never before had the impact of it hit me. God had chosen me? ME? ME! An insignificant housewife from Glasgow. I'm reminded of the words of a song I have often sung, 'Who am I?'

> Who am I that a king should bleed and die for?
> Who am I that he should pray, not my will but thine for?
> The answer I may never know, why he ever loved me so
> That to an old rugged cross he would go
> For who am I?
> (Charles [Rusty] Goodman)

Moses asked the question when God confronted him and told him that he had chosen him to go and set his people free from their bondage in Egypt. **WHO AM I?** I struggled with my identity in Christ for a number of years until I realised that God loved ME and in his eyes I was special. I think the Apostle Peter wrote his first epistle to encourage people like me!

In Acts 16:2 Claudius, the Roman Emperor, banished all the Jews from Rome, and they had to scatter and disperse all over Asia Minor to find refuge and preserve their lives. Some of them saw their family members and friends murdered and imprisoned for life for the sake of the gospel. They lost everything and were strangers in a foreign land.

The background of the writing of the epistle of Peter is interesting. Peter wrote it about AD 64 and it is the last epistle he wrote prior to his arrest and imprisonment by Nero, and it was during that time that he wrote his second epistle. Somewhere close to AD 68 Peter was finally martyred, crucified upside down. According to tradition he didn't feel worthy to be crucified like his Lord and Saviour Jesus Christ. Peter is called the Apostle of hope, John the Apostle of love and Paul the Apostle of faith. In writing this epistle Peter was giving hope to hopeless, suffering people, and so we find that eighteen times he uses the words 'suffer' and 'suffering' and eight times he uses the word 'grace'.

As we travel through life, all of us will encounter suffering in one way or another. It may be through ill health, bereavement, financial problems, marriage problems or rebellious children. **BUT GOD** by his unique grace gives us hope, as we discover from this wonderful epistle.

The Apostle Paul suffered many trials as he walked his Christian path. He talked about his thorn in the flesh which he asked God to remove, **BUT GOD** did not answer his request the way Paul would have liked him to, instead, God told him that His strength would be made perfect in his weakness and that his grace would be sufficient to see him through his suffering. Paul's hope was in the provision of God's amazing powerful grace. Barbara Johnson, author of *Splashes of Joy in the Cesspools of Life,* says, 'The day the Lord created hope was probably the day He created springtime.'

The Apostle Peter opens up his first epistle with *hope.*

This letter was sent out all over Asia Minor where there were little groups of believers who were suffering and going through difficult times because they had lost their identity. When this epistle came it gave them hope.

The first thing Peter says to them is that what they have to understand is that they are chosen according to the foreknowledge of God, even though they were strangers in the land.

They also have to understand that they are God's by the sanctifying work of the Holy Spirit, and that grace and peace is theirs in fullest measure.

What a wonderful God, we can praise and worship him because...

> we have a new birth and a living hope;
> we have an inheritance that will not fade away;
> we have a faith that is found in the power of God;
> and we can rejoice in our trials;
> we rejoice in eternal salvation that will be culminated in the coming again of the Lord Jesus Christ;
> in our trials, our faith is more genuine and valuable than refined gold and our faith brings us inexpressible joy.

Even though we live in a world surrounded by idolatry, impurity and discord, our hope is that we are God's elect, God's chosen ones, sanctified by the Holy Spirit. And we have grace and peace in abundance. However, there may be times when life is really difficult and the truth of all that seems like a dream! A woman dreamt that the Lord had come and everything was wonderful. Then she woke up, turned on the news and it just spoiled everything!

In *The Gospel according to Peanuts*, Lucy and Charlie Brown were going through the shopping precinct (mall) and Lucy saw a fountain. She said to Charlie, 'If you throw a coin into that fountain and make a wish, your wish will be granted.' 'Let's do it,' said Charlie. 'Now you have to tell your wish out loud,' Lucy told him. 'Do I have to?' asked Charlie. 'Yes.' said Lucy. She went over to the fountain and threw in her coin and said, 'I wish I had a new sweater, a new pair of skates and lots of money.' Charlie Brown threw his coin into the fountain and said, 'I wish that there was peace in the world and there would be no more hunger, suffering and sorrow.' Lucy looked at him with disgust and as she walked away she said, 'Charlie Brown, you sure do know how to spoil everything.' Material things mattered to Lucy, but Charlie saw beyond the material and longed for more than selfish desires. That was probably what touched Lucy's conscience and spoiled things for her.

The reason Peter wrote to these scattered people was to enable them to live in hope in a hopeless situation. How to do this is found in verse nine. '[Y]ou may declare the praises of him who called you out of darkness into his wonderful light' (1 Pet. 2:9). Peter begins by telling his readers that they have hope because they are God's elect, even though they are strangers in the land. They are God's chosen ones according to the very foreknowledge of God. They have to understand that they are God's people, sanctified by the work of the Holy Spirit. Because of God's abundant grace and peace they could praise and worship him, finding in him all they could need.

Praise is more than meets the eye. When many of us think of praise we think of singing or lifting their hands.

Or we think of the great atmosphere of the 'worship' service. But when the Bible talks about praise it is far more than that. In reality praise is the very reason for the existence of the whole universe. Everything we see, God created for praise. When the daffodils and blossom come out in the spring, they sing the praise of God. When the sun shines down in its brilliance in the summer, it sings praise to God. When the leaves put on their beautiful show in the autumn, they sing praise to God. When the snow caps the mountains in winter, it sings praise to God.

I believe this is what David is saying in Psalm 148:7-10 when he says, 'Praise the LORD from the earth, you great sea creatures and all ocean depths, lightning and hail, snow and clouds, stormy winds that do his bidding, you mountains and all hills, fruit trees and all cedars, wild animals and all cattle, small creatures and flying birds …' The whole earth sings one song of praise to the One who is Creator, Sustainer and Redeemer.

When we begin to understand praise, we begin to understand what our primary role is. Our very being is centred on the fact that we bring praise to God. 'Man's chief end is to glorify God and praise Him forever' (*The Shorter Catechism*).

But how do we live a life of praise to God? I believe this is what Peter is referring to when he wrote to these people who were scattered without identity and with no hope, and he would say the same to us today. He tells them that they have to understand who they really are. Their problem was that they really did not know who they were. Who am I? How do I see myself? Jessie McFarlane, speaker, secretary of Moldova Ministries, founder of Prayer Chain Ministries, or a member of such and such a church?

Within a space of two weeks I met people from very different backgrounds. One group were wives of Members of Parliament when I spoke to them in Westminster, London. The other group were from the poorest countries in Eastern Europe. Materially they had nothing. Neberna came to the AD2000 Conference with one skirt and one blouse, and yet all of these people had one thing in common, they all knew who they were in Christ! Peter tells these hopeless people, and us, this is who you are. You are a chosen people, a royal priesthood, a holy nation; you are a people belonging to God.

A CHOSEN PEOPLE?

What does Peter mean when he says that you are a chosen people? We are chosen, first and foremost, to glorify God and part of the way in which we do that is to be witnesses and ambassadors for Jesus Christ. Israel, as a nation, was given the responsibility of witnessing to the world. The church, as the kingdom of God on earth, has also been given the responsibility of witnessing to the modern world. We have been commissioned by God to 'go and make disciples of all nations' (Matt. 28:19). But how can we do this effectively? In Matthew 16:18-19 Jesus said, 'I will build my church; and the gates of hades will not overcome it. I will give you the keys of the kingdom of heaven; whatever you bind on earth will be bound in heaven, and whatever you loose on earth will be loosed in heaven.'

Jesus entrusted the keys of the kingdom to the early disciples. On Peter's confession that Jesus was the

Christ, the Son of the Living God, Jesus gave him and others who would follow incredible authority for the purpose of spreading the work of His kingdom here on earth. As the early Church in the book of Acts grew, *prayer and witness* went hand in hand as the Holy Spirit worked through the disciples.

Jesus gave Peter a key on the day of Pentecost and Peter went forward in obedience and opened the door of the church to 3,000 new believers (Acts 2:41). Jesus gave Stephen a key; Stephen obeyed and walked into a martyr's death, but influenced Paul who became the greatest soul-winner of the early church (Acts 7). Jesus gave a key to Philip who opened the door to the Samaritans and also another key that took him into the desert, and on the Gaza road the door was opened to the Ethiopian Church and to Africa. The disciples prayed, preached and witnessed and God built His Church, not of brick and mortar, but of living stones, those who have acknowledged that they are sinners before a Holy God and accepted Jesus Christ as their Lord and Saviour.

I have referred to the involvement my husband Peter and I have in Moldova. God is certainly building his Church there, not only of brick and mortar, but also more importantly of living stones. At present Moldova Ministries is building their sixth church. Bethany Church, built five years ago, has now outgrown their present building and a new church is almost completed which will seat 800–1,000 people. Just a few months ago seventeen young people, new believers, were baptised, and each week sees men, women, boys and girls coming to faith in Jesus Christ.

Is it any wonder Peter and I say when we come back home, it's like shopping at Harrods and coming home to shop in Poundstrechers!

ROYAL PRIESTHOOD

The Apostle Peter also tells us that we are a Royal Priesthood. That puts us in a special status. We are called to be intercessors for the world. Yet is it not true that in many of our churches we are so introverted we cannot see beyond our own four walls? Prayer becomes almost like an online shopping list, *'our* Sunday school, *our* women's meeting, *our* pastor'. Please do not misunderstand me; it is not wrong to pray for these things, but where is our vision beyond 'our church'?

'Where there is no vision, the people perish' (Prov. 29:18 KJV). God's burden is for a lost world, and it should also be our burden. I found this adaptation of 1 Corinthians 13 and it has been very challenging.

> *Though I speak concerning foreign missions with great eloquence and have not vision, I am become as sounding brass and a tinkling symbol.*
>
> *And though I spend hours in study reading missionary literature and know much concerning the hardships and difficulties of a missionary's life and have no vision, it profits me nothing.*
>
> *A vision holds one steady before God, a vision enables one to pray earnestly, a vision gives a burden that many others may have salvation.*
>
> *It does not exalt any but Christ, it seeks only the redemption of the lost, it is given to those who earnestly seek it and thinks no price is too great to pay.*

It does not discourage those who would be missionaries, but encourages them to answer the call of God.

It bears one another's burdens, believes that God is willing to undertake, prays for the salvation of many and endures failure and disappointment.

A vision does not soon fade away, but when there is excitement of self-seeking it shall fail.

Where there are tears at a missionary convention they shall cease, where there is only interest it shall vanish away.

For all Christians know in part and all Christians see in part; but when they have a vision their apathy and intermittent interest shall be done away.

Before I caught the vision I spoke as one without a vision, I prayed as one without a vision, but when I caught the vision, I put away half-hearted things.

For now, at least I have caught a faint glimpse of the need, which Jesus alone can satisfy. But some day I shall realise it fully, now I know something of the price of salvation, but then I shall see it clearly, the cost of my salvation.

And now to be a Christian missionary, these are necessary…a prayerful heart, a surrendered life, a vision, these three with others, but one of the greatest is a vision.

Anon.

What a wonderful privilege it is when God gives us a vision from his heart to see men and women who are without Christ and on their way to a lost eternity. And what a privilege it is to stand in the gap and pray for the peace of Jerusalem, for God's chosen people, for the persecuted, for those living in war-torn countries, and for the hungry and homeless.

David Livingstone, the Scottish missionary and explorer, read these words by Robert Moffat: 'From where I stand I can see the smoke of 10,000 African villages who have never heard of Christ.' This ignited a vision in David Livingstone's heart. With faith in a faithful God he walked for miles through the African jungle, his Bible in his hand. He fought illness and wild animals, and he fought slavery until he won the heart of a nation. Livingstone was found dead on his knees in an obscure African village. All of this because he had a vision and was obedient to the call of God on his life.

Samuel Chadwich said, 'The world will never believe in a religion in which there is no power. A rationalised faith, a socialised church, and a moralised gospel may gain applause, but they awaken no conviction and gain no converts.'

The Church in Jerusalem started from small beginnings, just 120 believers, yet spread throughout the Roman Empire. They had no political clout, no friends in high places to 'pull strings' for them. They were a praying people and they went to the Highest Throne, the Throne of grace. They knew that God could solve their problems. They were a praying church. God works when churches pray. Satan still trembles when he sees the weakest sinner on his knees.

I have found that prayerlessness is powerlessness. When I don't have prayer power, I don't have God power! Sam Shoemaker said, 'Some people have enough of religion to make them feel uneasy in a gambling shop, but not enough to make them feel at home in a prayer meeting.' Samuel Chadwick states powerfully that, 'there is no power like that of prevailing prayer ... it turns ordinary mortals into men of power. It brings fire, it brings rain, it brings life, – it brings God.'

A Holy Nation

As I write, there is being advertised on television a programme to be viewed next week about the life of Mary Whitehouse, the English campaigner for decency in the media. The actress playing the role of Mary Whitehouse, Julie Walters, said that in the 1960s when she was a teenager she disliked Mrs Whitehouse as she was 'spoiling teenagers' fun'. But as she became involved in her role in the film, she now admires 'that woman' for exposing child abuse and bringing the 'watershed' to media. Mary Whitehouse was made a laughing stock by comedians and the butt of television jokes. Sadly, Christians in our nation did not stand with her in her fight against the filth coming into our homes through the television. The floodgates opened, and now we cannot stop the tide of blasphemy, pornography and evil penetrating our nation.

What does it mean to be a holy nation? Paul tells us in Philippians 3:20 that: 'We, however, are citizens of heaven, and we eagerly wait for our Saviour, the Lord Jesus Christ, to come from heaven' (*Good News Bible*). We have dual citizenship. We render to Caesar the things that are Caesar's. We do what we have to do to obey the laws of our land, but we have a higher law, a different set of rules, a different code. We belong to the kingdom of God.

Where is that kingdom? In Luke 17:21 Jesus says that the kingdom is in us. Paul tells us in Romans 14:17

that it is not eating and drinking, but that the kingdom we belong to is righteousness, peace and joy in the Holy Spirit. The knowledge that we are right with God gives us peace and joy. We should, therefore, be living holy lives and witnessing for the Lord, seeking to bring others into his kingdom.

The words of Jesus in Matthew 7:13-25 are extremely important and demand our attention. He talks about the small gate and narrow road, and the wide gate and broad road. Someone has explained that these roads are like a wide motorway with a narrow road going down the middle and the people on the narrow road going in the opposite direction. When we repent of our sin and accept Jesus Christ as our Lord we are on the narrow road. Our lives have been changed; we no longer should live like the world. Paul tells us that 'if anyone is in Christ, he is a new creation; the old has gone, the new has come!'(2 Cor. 5:17). We are on the road to being made holy. '[B]ecause by one sacrifice he has made perfect for ever those who are being made holy' (Heb. 10:14). If we know Jesus Christ, and he has by his Spirit come into our lives, he will do everything in his power to see that we keep on the narrow road. I thank God for the many occasions he has pulled me back to the narrow road, when I could have made wrong choices, and been sidetracked back into the world. **BUT GOD** by his wonderful grace kept me and used the experiences to teach me more about his great faithfulness.

Peter then goes on to say that we are a people belonging to God. What does that mean? We are told in 1 Corinthians 6:19-20, 'that your body is a temple of the Holy Spirit, who is in you, whom you have received from God? You are not your own; you were bought at a price. Therefore honour God with your body.'

There is something very interesting here. You can take ordinary things and when they belong to someone important they take on great value. In the Elvis Presley museum in America, there is an automobile that belonged to Elvis Presley, which would sell for $2,000 in the open market, but because it belonged to Elvis Presley it is worth $1,000,000. In Sir Winston Churchill's home there is a beautiful model of a ship made of burnt-out matches. If I had made this it would be worth nothing, but because it belonged to Sir Winston Churchill it is of great value.

When Peter says we are a people belonging to God, we are special, because we were bought at great cost. It cost the Son of God everything. He left the glories of heaven and came to planet earth. He was hated, abused and crucified by the men he had created, so that we could belong to God. We should never underestimate ourselves. It is not what we have in material possessions, but who we are in Christ, and because we belong to him that we are worth more than anything else in the world! You are special because there is not another person like you on earth! Once we grasp this we begin to know who and what we are.

Not only did Peter say who we are, and what we are, but he also goes on to say that we have to determine how we are going to live. And it is only when we know who we are that we can do that.

The story is told of a little girl who came to her mother and asked, where did I come from? The answer her mother gave her was 'God sent you.' The little girl thought for a moment and said, 'Did God send you?' 'Yes,' her mother said. 'Did God send Grandma?' 'Yes,' said her mother. 'Did God send great grandma?' 'Yes,' her mother said. The little girl was very thoughtful and then she said, 'That's really strange. We haven't had a natural birth in this family for over 200 years.'

Once we know who we really are and where we've come from we can decide how to live.

Peter says, here's who you are – a chosen people. Here's what you are – Royal priesthood, a holy nation. Here's your value – a people belonging to God, who declare the praises of him who called you out of darkness into his wonderful light.

Beginning with verse 11 we have to determine how we are going to live, on the basis of who we are, and here is how Peter instructs us. We have to *live clean lives* (1 Pet. 2:11-12). Abstain from sinful desires that war against your soul, sinful desires that Satan uses in a pagan system today. Whether we want to accept it or not, pagans are in control of our nation. There is little awareness or recognition of God. We can relate to Isaiah's cry in chapter 59, especially verses 12-15. 'For our offences are many in your sight, and our sins testify against us. Our offences are ever with us, and we acknowledge our iniquities: rebellion and treachery against the LORD, turning our back on our God, fomenting oppression and revolt, uttering lies our hearts have conceived. So justice is driven back, and righteousness stands at a distance; truth has stumbled in the streets, honesty cannot enter. Truth is nowhere to be found, and whoever shuns evil becomes a prey.'

Pagans are in control of the judicial system; they have economic control, educational control and social control. It was the same in Peter's day. Rome was a pagan nation, and it had Asia Minor in its clutches of immorality. But Peter says it doesn't matter what laws the judiciary passes, the Christian lives by God's law, that law that we find in Exodus 20. God wants us to live by his standards as his children. We have to live clean lives.

The second thing he says in verse 12 is that we have to *be courageous.* Some of the greatest testimonies in the world today are those of people of God who live courageous lives. More people could be touched by the lifestyle of courageous Christians than may be touched by sermons preached. It may be that the greatest evangelistic movement to touch our nations will take place when the church doors swing open and we go out into the marketplace and live Christlike lives. When we do that all eyes will be on us. I read somewhere of a pastor who placed a notice on the gate leaving the church which read: 'You are now entering the mission field.' When we live under the anointed courage of the Lord, our witness will be blessed and effective.

Peter continues to encourage us in verse 13 to *live commendable lives*. I understand that during the Communist regime, 50,000 pastors were imprisoned for their faith. One such pastor was imprisoned for twenty-two years. While in prison he lived a commendable consistent life. When he came out of prison, twenty-six men came out with him, who, through his witness, had accepted Christ, and are now pastors.

One young man said that they used to do everything to make him give up his faith. He spent seven years of his twenty-two years in solitary confinement because of the things they did to him. But they saw him live a consistent life regardless of the torture, regardless of the injustice, sickness and privation. They saw him miraculously raised up time after time from the jaws of death. A young man said, 'If that man's faith brings that kind of power, I want that faith. I came to know Jesus Christ because that man lived a commendable life before us.' The world today does not read or believe the Bible, but it is reading us. How are we portraying Christ to the world?

Fourthly, in verse 17 we are called to live a *committed life*. 'Honour all people, love God, and honour the king.' Love is the greatest power we have. If a church really reflects God, it reflects love because the heart of God is love. 'For God so loved the world that he gave his one and only Son, that whoever believes in him shall not perish but have eternal life' (John 3:16). I suspect that nothing causes more laughter in hell and more tears in heaven than when Christians do not love one another.

Lastly, and most importantly, we have to live *Christlike lives*, verses 21-25. We have been called for this purpose, since Christ also suffered for us, leaving us an example to follow in the steps of the One who committed no sin, nor was any deceit found in his mouth; and while being reviled he did not revile in return; while suffering, he uttered no threats, but kept entrusting himself to God who judges righteously (1 John 1).

I'm so glad that Peter wrote to these people who had lost their hope, because I need to constantly be reminded of who I am, what I am and my value to God.

I don't know where it comes from, but I love this story because it reflects practical love. One cold winter's day a ten-year-old boy was standing barefoot in front of a shoe store, peering through the window and shivering with cold. A lady approached the boy and asked him what he was doing.

'I was asking God to give me a pair of shoes,' the boy replied.

The lady took him by the hand, went into the store and asked the assistant to get a half dozen pairs of socks for the boy. She then asked for a basin of hot water and a towel. The shop assistant quickly brought them to her. The woman took the boy to the back of the store, knelt down, washed his little feet and dried them with a towel, by this time the assistant returned with the socks. Placing one pair on the boy's feet, she then purchased him a pair of shoes. Then tying up the remaining pairs of socks, she gave them to him. The woman patted the boy on the head and said, 'I'm sure, my little fellow you feel more comfortable now.' As she turned to go, the astonished lad caught her by the hand, and looking up into her face with tears in his eyes, answered the question with these words, 'Are you God's wife?'

Some years ago, as a family we went on a caravanning holiday to Denmark. We worshipped in a Brethren Assembly in Copenhagen where we met a dear godly lady, Miss Edith English. She was seventy-three when we met her and the following year she came and spent two weeks in our home. It was the first time in her life she had been on a plane. 'Aunt Edith', as she became affectionately known, was God's gift to us at a crucial time in our children's lives. She had discernment and understanding and gave us of her wisdom.

I remember one beautiful day. When I took her breakfast to her I said that it would be a lovely day to sit in the garden. She thanked me, and said, 'Jessie, I need to spend the morning with the Lord.' As I was a young mum with four children, and I found little time to spend with the Lord, I said to her, 'Aunt Edith, I look forward to getting old, so that I can spend more time with the Lord.' Her answer took me by surprise. 'Jessie, believe me, it doesn't get any easier.'

Now a little older than Aunt Edith, I understand what she meant. It doesn't get easier. Sometimes, the knocks you get in life shatter your confidence, especially when they come from fellow Christians. Tiredness seems to sap your energy and everything takes longer to do. It is at this point Satan would love to see us down and keep us down. **BUT GOD** comes to us and by his wonderful powerful grace, he reminds us that we are chosen, that we are of value to him and in his eyes we are special. Someone has paraphrased what Paul says in Galatians 4:7: 'You are God's child and God will give you the blessing he promised, because you are his child.'

I don't know who wrote this lovely poem, but it has been a blessing to me.

You are who you are for a reason,
You're part of an intricate plan.
You're a precious and perfect unique design,
Called God's special woman or man.

You look like you look for a reason,
Our God made no mistake.

He knit you together within the womb,
You're just what he wanted to make.

The parents you had were the ones he chose,
And no matter how you may feel,
They were custom-designed with God's plan in mind
And they bear the Master's seal.

No, that trauma you faced was not easy
And God wept that it hurt you so;
But it was allowed to shape your heart,
so that into his likeness you'd grow.

You are who you are for a reason
You've been formed by the Master's rod,
You are who you are, beloved,
because you're a child of God.
(Russell Kelfer)

I started reading books on prayer. Three in particular spoke to me: Evelyn Christenson's *What Happens When Women Pray?* and Dick Eastman's *The Hour that Changes the World* and *No Easy Road*. An adventure was about to begin with a steep learning curve. My whole concept of prayer had been mistaken. It was not, I discovered, the carrying of a shopping list to the great supermarket in the sky. Nor was it a divine problem page. Prayer was much wider than anything I had imagined. But there were conditions attached to it. God showed me that I had been coming into his holy presence with unclean hands and an impure heart. I had an attitude problem. 'If I had cherished sin in my heart, the Lord would not have listened' (Ps. 66:18). I began to understand more about the holiness of God and about the state of heart and mind I needed to have in order even to begin to approach him.

One prayer I had prayed for many years was that I would die before my father did. I loved him so very deeply. But how true it is that God's answers are always wiser than our prayers. When we came home from holiday in July 1972, I visited my parents. Dad's words to me as I left were the last I was to hear him speak on earth. 'As for me,' he testified, 'I will behold thy face in righteousness; I shall be satisfied, when I awake, with thy likeness' (Ps. 17:15, AV). That was Sunday. Dad died on Wednesday.

For nine days after his death I lived in an empty world. No one came to comfort. There were no phone calls and not one letter of sympathy arrived. We had a wide circle of friends but nobody seemed to care. In my despair I read Oswald Chamber's *My Utmost for His Highest*.

> You have been to Jordan over and over again with Elijah, but now you are up against it alone. It is no use saying you cannot go; the experience has come and you must go. If you want to know whether God is the God you have faith to believe him to be, then go through your Jordan alone.

I began to understand. I needed people, I didn't know who I was and I found my personhood in how other people saw me. I wanted to be liked. In my extremity God taught me a lesson. I did not need props. God could be the one and only foundation of my life. And I realised then that this was a truth God would have me know, whether with my willing compliance or despite myself. It was years later Peter told me that he had seen a change in my life that dated from that black and bleak experience.

A change there was, but that did not mean life became a bed of roses. There were thorns aplenty. The periods between my father's death and my mother's death six years later were busy ones indeed. I did all the things a wife and mother had to do while trying to spend more time with my own mother who needed me. Have you ever seen a juggler? That was me. If a juggler loses his concentration he loses control. There were times when I was so busy concentrating on keeping everything else going that I failed in the very things that mattered most. We often make the excuse that we have no time.

Here is another poem which also has been a blessing to me over the years.

> You who are beyond time Lord, you smile to see us fighting it
> And you know what you are doing.
> You make no mistakes in your distribution of time to me.
> You give to each one time to do what you want him to do.
> But we must not lose time, waste time, or kill time.
> For time is a gift that you gave us.
> But a perishable gift, a gift that does not keep
> Lord, I have time, I have plenty of time
> All the time you gave me. The years of my life
> The days of my years, the hours of my days.
> They are all mine.
> Mine to fill quietly, calmly,
> But to fill completely, up to the brim.

To offer them to you, that of their inspired water,
You may make a rich wine,
Such as you made once in Cana of Galilee
I am not asking Lord for time to do this and then that.
But your grace to do conscientiously in the time that
   you give me,
WHAT YOU WANT ME TO DO?
(Michel Quoist)

I think one of the saddest things we can experience in old age is to look back and realise that we have settled for a second-rate life, taking no risks, playing it safe.

Max Lucado writes in his book *He Still Moves Stones*: 'Jesus says the options are clear. On the one side there is the voice of safety. You can build a fire in the hearth and stay warm, dry and safe. You can't get hurt if you never get out. You can't be criticised for what you don't try. You can't fall if you don't take a stand. You can't lose your balance if you never climb. So don't try it. Take the safe route. Or you can hear the voice of adventure – God's adventure. Instead of building a fire in your hearth, build a fire in your heart. Follow God's impulses...Make a difference, sure it isn't safe, but what is?'

My husband Peter, a few years before he retired, was invited to go to Moldova, where God lit a fire in his heart which has burned now for nineteen years. He left his comfort zone to take the gospel to folks who had lost their hope. At the age of eighty-one he is still travelling to Moldova, and has more vision than he has years left to fulfil. You can read Peter's story later in the book.

J.C. Penney, when he was ninety-five years old, said that his eyesight was getting weaker, but his vision was increasing. When I think of the potential in the lives of older believers it saddens me that this potential is rarely tapped. Churches would be much the better from releasing the wisdom and knowledge of these people to be mentors to younger men and women.

No, it doesn't get any easier, but thank God that, like the Psalmist in Psalm 118:13-14, we can say without hesitation, 'I was pushed back and about to fall, but the LORD helped me. The LORD is my strength and my song; he has become my salvation.' The demands of life today often leave us little time to fulfil all we would desire to do for God. Maybe we should evaluate our schedule and learn to live by priorities. It is strange that we always find time to have coffee with friends, read our favourite magazine and watch television!

When twenty-four hours in a day are not enough, remember this story of a jar of mayonnaise and two cups of coffee. I don't know where this came from, but it's good.

> A professor stood before his philosophy class and had some items in front of him. When the class began, he wordlessly picked up a very large and empty mayonnaise jar and proceeded to fill it with golf balls. He then asked the students if the jar was full. They agreed it was. The professor then picked up a box of pebbles and poured them into the jar. He shook the jar lightly. The pebbles rolled into the open areas between the golf balls. He then asked the students again if the jar was full. They agreed it was.

> The professor next picked up a box of sand and poured it into the jar. Of course the sand filled up everything else. He asked once more if the jar was full. The students responded with a unanimous 'Yes'.

Then the professor then produced two cups of coffee from under the table and poured the entire contents into the jar, effectively filling the empty space between the sand. The students laughed.

'Now,' said the professor, as the laughter subsided, 'I want you to recognize that this jar represents your life. The golf balls are the important things – God, your family, your children, your health, your friends and your favourite passions – and if everything else was lost and only they remained, your life would still be full. The pebbles are the other things that matter like your job, your house and your car. The sand is everything else – the small stuff. If you put the sand into the jar first,' he continued, 'there is no room for the pebbles or the golf balls. The same goes for life. If you spend all your time and energy on the small stuff you will never have room for the things that are important to you. Pay attention to the things that are critical to your happiness. Play with your children. Take time to get medical check-ups. Take your spouse out to dinner. Play another 18 holes of golf. There will always be time to clean the house and fix the disposal. Take care of the golf balls first – the things that really matter. Set your priorities. The rest is just sand!'

One of the students raised her hand and inquired what the coffee represented. The professor smiled. 'I'm glad you asked. It just goes to show you that no matter how full your life may seem, there's always room for a couple of cups of coffee with a friend!'

I needed to get my priorities right!

Bible reading was again pushed into spare minutes and specific times of prayer grew less frequent. And when that happened I lost control. Prone as I was to depression, Satan was never far from whispering things in my ear to discourage me and get me down. Because I was not always attuned to the voice of God, I heard what Satan was saying and believed him. I was a failure, he convinced me of that. And to avoid the criticism I was sure I was due, I withdrew, even from Peter. Only the children could take me out of myself. How I wish I had known then what I know now. God breaks us, but only to encourage new and beautiful growth.

I have written in the flyleaf of my Bible this beautiful prayer by Phillip Brooks. 'O Lord, by all Your dealings with us, whether of joy or pain, of light or darkness, let us be brought to You. Let us value no treatment of Your grace simply because it makes us happy or because it makes us sad, because it gives us or denies us what we want. But may all that You send us bring us to You, that knowing Your perfectness, we may be sure in every disappointment that You are still loving us, and in every darkness that You are still enlightening us, and in every enforced idleness that You are still using us. Yes, in every death that You are still giving us life, as in His death You gave life to Your Son our Saviour, Jesus Christ' (From *Reflections on Prayer*, Into Thy Word Ministries).

Even the tears we shed when he lays his hand heavily upon us refresh and water. None of God's dealings are for our harm. He is making us company fit for the King of kings. Satan's aim is to destroy us and he will use every trick in the book to do it. The two weapons he used most effectively in my life were the undermining of my confidence and the filling of my life so full that it was easy to let times of personal devotion slip. He also made me dissatisfied.

Compared with my life Peter's seemed so interesting. Shortly after moving to Bishopbriggs there was a proposal to open a prison in the area. Opposition was predictably strong and noisy. However, after some time, the prison authorities won the argument and Low Moss Prison was established. As Peter had a burden for the men held in custody there, he approached the Governor with the suggestion that he should take a Bible class each Sunday for the prisoners. The Governor was not bursting with enthusiasm, but neither did he dismiss the idea totally. Six months later, when Peter approached him for a second time, the answer was a quite definite, 'Thank you, but no thank you.'

Bishopbriggs boasts its own local newspaper and it was in it that Peter noticed a report of the farewell dinner for Low Moss Prison's Governor. It was not long before he approached his successor. Midway through his conversation with him, the new Governor, Mr William McVey, held out his hand to Peter, 'Put your hand there, brother,' he smiled, 'when do you want to start?'

So began Peter's work with prisoners, a work which was to bring him alongside prisoners and prison staff for many years and through which he had the privilege of presenting the gospel to people who not only needed to hear it, but who knew more than most of us that they were in need. But it was not easy.

Having been brought up in the Maryhill area of Glasgow, Peter went into prison work with his eyes open. He was no starry-eyed idealist whose evangelical feet had long since left the ground. Peter had helped to scrape drunkards off the pavement as a lad, he had seen poverty and deprivation although his own family had never been in want. And he knew at first hand what it was to experience violence in his home, thankfully rarely, and only as a result of his father's very occasional alcoholic binges. Converted, like me, at the age of eleven, by the time Peter was an adult he was well schooled in life. Further training was forthcoming, and from an unconventional university. When an inmate he met at the Low Moss Bible Class was released from prison he came to stay in our home for a short time.

When Peter tried to discuss his difficulties with him his efforts met with the reply, 'Look, Peter, you are not going to understand me until you have been where I have been.' 'Well,' my husband responded, 'I have not been where you have been, but if there are places you could take me that would help me to understand, then I am happy to go.' 'Yes,' he was told, 'there are. I'll take you to places.'

Peter went out with him several winter evenings. I will never forget the first time Peter came home after a visit with Alistair. His words to me were, 'I've been to hell and back'. They went to places together that Peter did not know existed. He was taken to a hideout where our friend had hidden, along with another criminal, for six months to escape detection by the police, and from which they had gone out night after night to mug and rob. While they were there the man's criminal colleague arrived and Peter was clearly bad news. It was only his friend's less than accurate explanation that Peter was a priest who was trying to help that prevented a tense situation becoming decidedly ugly.

A young tramp took Peter into another classroom of life. He had been a professional soldier when his wife became ill and died. Unable to cope, before long he was discharged from the army, took to drink and became a tramp, all by the age of thirty. Peter tried to help him with accommodation when he was released. He said he was OK, he had somewhere he could go. For several months before his last arrest he had lived in a derelict building in the centre of Glasgow (tramps call this skippering), and he went back there to stay.

The following evening when they met up, he asked Peter if he saw anything different about him. He was pleased when my husband noticed that he had on another shirt. He had gone to Paddie's Market, Glasgow's notorious street market where clothes can be bought, sold and exchanged, and exchanged his old shirt for another one. That was the beginning of his journey up. Three days later, about six o'clock in the morning, our phone rang. Peter answered it. His former tramp not only had a new shirt, he had a new life. During the night, he explained excitedly to a now wide-awake Peter, he had received Christ as his Saviour. The skipper had become a temple, a palace. He said it had lit up and that his life had lit up too. His light is still shining today.

Among the inmates Peter met two men with whom he had gone to school. All three were brought up in the same area. They attended the same school and they had played football as members of the same team. Yet, they were behind bars and Peter was free. Situations like that moved him deeply and increased his resolve to reach out with the good news to men whose lives were bad news for themselves and for their families. Peter's maxim was, 'Remember those in prison as if you were their fellow prisoners, and those who are ill-treated as if you yourself were suffering.' When Peter met his former playmates he knew how easily he could have ended up on the same side of the bars as they were.

From time to time Peter came home with stories that warmed my heart. On one occasion the speaker he had invited to address the Bible class brought a friend along with him. Peter had never met his friend and had no time to get to know him before the class met. The guest speaker asked the stranger to talk to the men. He was a small man with an acute nasal problem which affected his speech. Within minutes the inmates became restless and the talk was punctuated by laughter.

Peter still remembers his embarrassment and bewilderment at his friend's choice of a speaker. But he recalls too how the restlessness calmed and the laughter stopped as the man's story unfolded. His description of childhood abuse reached the hearts of his hearers, many of whom could relate to his experience. Eyes shone with tears as they nodded in recognition and empathy. When he had spoken, the officer in charge, who always attended but was not the kind of man to get close to, walked forward and mounted the platform. He spoke right into the ear of the speaker, and the words Peter overheard were these, 'Bobby, you have found what I am searching for. Don't lose it.' When the prison officer left the platform he was crying.

Along with his prison ministry each Monday night our home housed thirty to forty young people who had been converted at an evangelistic campaign in Glasgow's Tent Hall. Peter had the joy of teaching them the truths of God's Word. These teenagers not only brought themselves, they also brought some unwelcome visitors which was why we bought a suite we could wash down and disinfect – and which would not harbour fleas!

When Peter's ministry extended into a whole new area, my life seemed so dull in comparison. One man he met was a gypsy and a drunk. He was a regular at Low Moss. Having said 'Cheerio' at the Bible class one Sunday he was liable to be there with a 'hello' a few weeks later. A shy man, a loner, who sat at the back of the class and kept himself at a distance from his fellow inmates, he was converted and after his release went, along with his mother, to live in a house for the first time in his life. None of his known generations had ever lived in a house. The former drunkard grew in grace and it was not long before he led his mother to the Lord. Such was his witness that many of his relatives also came to faith. Through him Peter was introduced to the gypsy culture and became accepted within it. Every Monday night for two years he held a Bible class for between thirty and forty gypsies, most of them new converts.

Even though I envied Peter his interesting ministry, his contacts and the importance of what he was doing, I was not blind to the discouragements he faced. The

Lord told a story about a sower sowing seed. Some of the seed was plucked up by birds before it had even begun to take root. Over and over again Peter saw that happen in his prison ministry. Men in whom there was a willingness, even a desperation for something better, heard the gospel but it seemed to be plucked away before it had any time to affect them. Some men were like the other seed in Jesus' story. The gospel appeared to take root in the solitude of prison but on release the flimsy seedlings died off, killed by the calamities of debt, disgrace and drink.

I listened to Peter's 'ups' and while often my heart warmed, sometimes the devil used these times to make me feel unsettled and dissatisfied. I listened to his 'downs' and wondered if at last he knew how I was feeling. Karen was eight years old when I rebelled. Peter had done all sorts of interesting things, now, I told him, it was my turn. I wanted a job. Had I thought it through I would have realised I was doing the only job I was really qualified to do – being a housewife! 'No,' said Peter firmly, 'you're not going out to work.' My friends found jobs or went to college to retrain and here was I, stuck at home. My dissatisfaction grew into resentment as Peter said 'No' to all my job suggestions. I never thought of asking God what he wanted to do with my life, or what his plans were for me. No wonder I was unhappy.

I had accumulated some stock phrases Peter could have put to music. 'I do the same old job day in and day out', would probably have been the melody. And the counterpoint would have provided, 'I'm stuck in a domestic rut', and 'I get no thanks for all I do.' What discord! Someone has said that insanity is doing the same thing the same way and expecting something different. Well, that something different seemed a long way off!

BUT GOD chose an interesting way to change the tune. One day I turned on the television to divert me from my morbid thoughts. Dr Donald Coggan was to be made Archbishop of Canterbury the following day and he was being interviewed. 'What do you think about all the pomp and circumstance surrounding your coronation?' he was asked.

His answer nearly blew my socks off! 'Whatever you do,' he replied, 'whether you're a housewife baking a cake or being crowned as Archbishop, it is all for the glory of God.' God being glorified in housework!! My heavenly Father spoke to me loud and clear. I asked his forgiveness, gave him my pent-up frustrations and prayed for his will to be done in my life.

A year later I was pregnant. It took a little while to get used to the idea, but when I did, life took on a new perspective. Housework, keeping our home clean and tidy, not for the pride of it but for the glory of God, became a joy rather than a burden. Kirsteen-Anne, our little bonus from the Lord, was born in July 1970, and what joy she brought with her. Shona was thirteen, Graham eleven and Karen nine. And they loved her.

5

No small beginning

There's no easy path to glory
There's no rosy road to fame
Prayer, no matter how you view it
Is no simple parlour game!

In 1978 I prayed a prayer, and God's answer to that prayer changed my life. 'Lord,' I begged, 'teach me to pray.' And he did. Here are some thoughts on the prayer Jesus taught his disciples, which have helped and encouraged me in prayer.

The disciples were men of prayer, devout Jews who had been taught to pray. As they watched Jesus in prayer, then saw him walk the consular roads of Palestine and do miracles, they must have realized that it was his nights, days and hours spent in prayer that made the difference.

The disciples asked Jesus to teach them one thing, and that was 'to pray' not to teach them 'a' prayer. I'm sure that if I had been one of the disciples I would have asked him how to raise the dead, or make the blind to see. Jesus' answer to the disciple's request resulted in a wonderful exposition of prayer which we find in Matthew 6:5-15. It comes almost in the middle of our Lord's teaching on the beatitudes on murder, adultery, divorce and loving our enemies. It would seem that he knew that the only way we can live victorious lives is by prayer!

I believe that the prayer Jesus taught his disciples was not meant to be a repetitive prayer, but a skeleton on which we should build our prayers. It is not a substitute for our own prayers, but a guide for them. In less than sixty words Jesus gives us a masterpiece of every conceivable element of true prayer in a simple form that even a child could understand.

The theme of relationships is a theme that dominates Scripture. Dr Larry Crabb says, 'From Genesis to Revelation the fabric of Biblical truth is woven with the thread of relationships, the perfect relationships in the Trinity, the broken relationships in Eden and the restored relationships in Christ. We are designed in our inner being for relationships – relationship with God and relationship with others.'

The prayer the Lord taught his disciples could be broken into five parts.

1. Relationship, then three responsibilities:
2. Glorifying God's Name
3. Extending His kingdom
4. Obeying His will.
5. Requests

Relationship to God our Father and to God's family when outlined from our relationship with God we see:

Our Father ... Father/child relationship
Hallowed be Thy name ... Deity/worshipper relationship

Thy kingdom come ... Sovereign/subject relationship
Thy will be done ... Master/servant relationship
Give us this day... Benefactor/beneficiary relationship
Forgive us our debts ... Saviour/sinner relationship
Do not lead us into temptation ... Guide/pilgrim relationship

Christianity is not a religion, but a relationship, and that relationship is to know God as our Father. We cannot know God as our Father unless we are born into his family. And we are born into the spiritual family of God by acknowledging that we are sinners, that is we have fallen short of God's standards and we are deserving his justice. **But God** has made provision for us to become his children through the death and resurrection of Jesus Christ, who 'bore our sins in his body on the tree' and paid the price for our salvation. When we pray we must have a right relationship with God through faith in Jesus Christ. Esther was brought into a relationship with the king, but the motive behind this relationship was not just to make her queen, which was responsibility enough, but also to be God's woman to save her people. She was 'brought to the kingdom for such a time as this' (*The Book of Esther*). We too are brought into God's kingdom to glorify God, and be witnesses for him.

The first of three responsibilities is to **hallow or glorify God's Name.** The supreme purpose in prayer is to glorify God, and he is concerned with the glory of his Name.

Jesus affirmed the purpose of prayer when he said, '[And] whatever you ask in my name, that will I do, [so] that the Father may be glorified' (John 14:13, NASB). This is what the Lord Jesus did while he was here on earth (John 12:28, John 17:4).

Much emphasis in the evangelical church today is on man's wants and needs. But true prayer is not to get man's will done in heaven, but to see God's will done on earth and to glorify His name. We can do nothing other than glorify God, when we understand who he is. To help us get to know his attributes it is good to do a study on the Names of God. Kay Arthur's book **Lord I want to Know You** is a helpful source of study on this subject.

Secondly we are to **hasten his kingdom.** The kingdom of God today is in the hearts of his believing people. We don't physically see God's kingdom here on earth, but we are promised that we shall one day, when Jesus returns. How can we be vital links in hastening this coming kingdom? Peter tells us in 2 Peter 3:11-12 (NASB) '...what sort of people ought you to be in holy conduct and godliness looking for and hastening the coming day of God...'. 'Therefore, beloved, since you look for these things, be diligent to be found by him in peace and blameless....' (v. 14, NASB) We should be living godly lives and witnessing for him in sharing the gospel. If I pray 'Thy kingdom come' and I am not living a godly life, I'm a hypocrite. If I pray Thy kingdom come and I'm not witnessing and seeking to bring others to Christ, I'm not obeying the command of the Lord Jesus in the Great Commission in Matthew 28:18: I'm a hypocrite.

Thirdly we are to **obey his will.** Prayer is not telling God what to do, it is finding out what he wants us to do and then asking him to accomplish his will through us. 'Unless the LORD builds the house, its builders labour in vain' (Ps. 127:1). God's will is clearly stated in Scripture. In Romans 12:2 we are instructed that we should present ourselves as a holy sacrifice to God in worship, we are not to be conformed to this world, but be transformed by the renewing of our minds, so that we might prove what the good, acceptable and perfect will of God is.

Paul prays for the Colossian believers that '[they] may be filled with the knowledge of his [God's] will in all spiritual wisdom and understanding, so that [they] will walk in a manner worthy of the Lord, to please him in all respects, bearing fruit in every good work and increasing in the knowledge of God' (Col. 1:9-10, NASB). When we have fulfilled the three responsibilities, then we can come with our requests and ask God for our daily bread, for forgiveness of our debts, for guidance and deliverance from temptation.

In *The Last Days Newsletter* Leonard Ravenhill tells about a group of tourists visiting a picturesque village who walked by an old man sitting beside a fence. In a rather patronizing way, one tourist asked, 'Were there any great men born in this village?' The old man replied, 'Nope, only babies!' No one is born a university graduate in the school of prayer. Prayer comes by practice and through being refined and shaped in the school of life. Oswald Chambers, one of my favourite writers, says, 'That when one is born from above, the life of the Son of God begins in him and he can either starve that life or nourish it. Prayer nourishes the life of God.'

The end of the Seventies was a learning time for me as circumstances threw me on the Lord. Nothing teaches us to pray quite so well as the absolute need to do so.

Satan's attacks in the past had been subtle, now they were vicious. My personal prayer times, which had been fitful, became urgent. Previously I had talked to God, now I clung to him. No longer did I bring a mental list of people to God for his blessing, I poured out my heart and soul to my Saviour. I particularly remember two days in which I knew God was doing a deep work in my life, two days when the Holy Spirit dealt with past hurts and showed wrong attitudes I had not surrendered to him. As I repented and confessed, God touched my life and I experienced the Holy Spirit in a new and special way.

My sister Wilma and I met regularly with our friend, Annette Dury, as a prayer triplet. We prayed for our families and friends, our congregations, and increasingly for our society. And as we prayed for our society the Lord seemed to increase our burden of concern for what was happening round about us. Family life in the United Kingdom was being devalued in so many ways, through the media, through legislation and, most of all, through neglect. And we were beginning to see the sad results of it in a generation of rootless young people.

Peter, meanwhile, was one of four men who invited the Argentinian evangelist, Luis Palau, to come to Glasgow in 1981 to hold a six-week-long mission. Two years of preparation went into his visit. During the early stages of their planning I felt a need to approach the preparation team and suggest that they should set up a covering of prayer for two weeks before the mission and for its duration. My recent experience of Satanic attack spoke loudly to me. If the devil was interested in mere me, how much more interested he would be in Luis Palau as he preached to many thousands of people. 'Why not share this with the prayer committee?' said Peter when I told him my thinking. Phoning the chairman, I suggested an eight week long, 24-hour day prayer clock for the mission. I am not quite sure what response I expected but the one I got was a surprise. 'OK Jessie, you organise it'. Now as a mother I gained a lot of organizational skills, but this was something else!

During a meeting in East Kilbride God spoke to me through a verse of Scripture. '[I]f my people, who are called by my name, will humble themselves and pray and seek my face and turn from their wicked ways, then will I hear from heaven and will forgive their sin and will heal their land. Now my eyes will be open and my ears attentive to the prayers offered in this place' (2 Chron. 7:14-15). I accepted the invitation to join the mission's Prayer Committee and arrange a prayer clock.

'"For I know the plans I have for you," declares the LORD, "plans to prosper you and not to harm you, plans to give you hope and a future."' This verse in Jeremiah 29:11 is very special. Isn't it wonderful to know that nothing takes God by surprise, that he has a purpose that involves the whole earth? In Isaiah 14:26-27 we read, 'This is the plan determined for the whole world; this is the hand stretched out over all nations. For the LORD Almighty has purposed, and who can thwart him? His hand is stretched out, and who can turn it back?' He is Sovereign and when he decides to do something, nothing can stop him. 'From the east I summon a bird of prey; from a far-off land, a man [*or woman*] to fulfil my purpose. What I have said, that will I bring about; what I have planned, that will I do' (Isa. 46:11).

When God was ready to judge the world he came to a man called Noah and Noah did all that God commanded him to do. He called Abraham to build the nation of Israel. He raised up Deborah to turn Israel back to himself, and when the fullness of time was come God sent his Son into the world. **But God knew all about 'prayer clocks', and he only had to plant a seed in my mind. He did the rest!**

The Lord guided in a wonderful way. Having divided each of the forty-eight days of the mission into forty-eight half-hour segments, I prepared sheets showing this in a graphic way. Then I contacted all the Christians I knew and asked them if they would be prepared to take a sheet showing the empty clock and fill it with people who would commit themselves to at least half an hour of prayer. And, just like Topsy, it grew and grew.

Blank clocks were passed from friend to friend and from church to church. People whose prayer lives had been vague found themselves being specific. Some whose busy lifestyles had pushed prayer into the background, as it had done in my own experience, were made aware of their priorities. And, to my amazement, several brothers and sisters in the Lord phoned from abroad to assure us that they were part of the mission's prayer clock and that they would be remembering us at their specific time. So it was that thousands of believing men and women, all over Scotland and beyond, spread a covering of prayer over the entire mission and rejoiced in the blessings God poured out on it.

Five thousand men, women, boys and girls were counselled and many responded to the call of the Spirit of God and gave their lives to Christ. Many blinded eyes were opened. One dear woman, who had read the Word of God and prayed for years with her mother and father, discovered that she had been reading and praying to a God she didn't know. Her eyes were opened and she found that this God wanted to be her personal Saviour and she found new life in Christ.

At one of the Crusade meetings, Luis quoted Isaiah 43:8, 'Lead out those who have eyes but are blind.' There was a woman in the audience to whom these verses came directly from the Lord. She had been brought up in a Christian home but rebelled against her upbringing. She became a nurse, married and had a family. Her husband died and her family married, leaving her very lonely. On the advice of a friend, she started taking a drink of wine at night to induce sleep. Sadly this became her downfall and she became an alcoholic. Through the help of friends and the A.A. she managed to struggle on until that night in the Kelvin Hall when Luis quoted that verse. Her eyes were opened to see the Saviour and she put her trust in him. Like the man in John 9, she could say, 'This one thing I know, I was blind, but now I can see.'

The mission over, Wilma, Annette and I continued to meet for prayer. Our concern for the nation grew as we looked around ourselves. The year 1981 seemed to us to mark an all-time low in the life of Britain. A long-distance lorry driver had just confessed to being the 'Yorkshire Ripper' and to having committed a series of appalling murders. Belfast had erupted in rioting after the death of their most famous hunger striker. Welsh miners were threatening to strike and the economic state of the nation was precarious. And the number of unemployed people in the country had risen to two and a half million. The Great Depression of the thirties was a folk memory to us rather than an actual one, but it was enough to make us aware of the dehumanising results of unemployment and the poverty that comes in its wake. We prayed for our nation.

'Evelyn Christenson's coming to speak in England,' said Wilma one day, just after the mission. 'I wonder why she's not coming up to Scotland.' We looked at the notice together. Scripture Press had arranged for her to speak at meetings in England and Ireland but none, so far as we could see, in Scotland. 'Why not phone and ask why she's not coming north,' I suggested. Wilma phoned. Scripture Press had, it seemed, tried to find a venue in Scotland but no one had been prepared to take it on so soon after the mission. We said we would. Five weeks was all we had to get it off the ground. We prayed. How we prayed. I think this was when I learned that God is not looking for capability so much as availability. We were available. **But God** knew the plans he had for us!

We booked Adelaide Place Baptist Church in Glasgow, all 1,200 seats of it! Humanly speaking, everything was against the meeting being a success. Many Christians in central Scotland were tired after the six-week-long Luis Palau campaign. They were looking forward to a holiday, not another meeting. We had no resources. Advertising was therefore limited to one advertisement in the Glasgow Herald and handouts in as many churches as we could reach. Evelyn Christenson was not known in Scotland, nor were her books widely read here. Having said that, I had bought many copies of *What Happens When Women Pray?* and given them to friends. I suspect they were passed on to others for none of them ever found their way home again.

June 22nd dawned. The meeting was scheduled to last from 10am until 4pm with a break for lunch. Wilma and I were there good and early. We stood inside the church looking at its 1,200 vacant seats. 'What have we done?' we asked each other. But by 10am 650 women had taken their seats, 650 women wanted to know what happens when women pray. **But God** knew the plans he had for Scotland and elsewhere!

Evelyn was quite different from the kind of speaker Scots women were used to. Aged sixty-four, she looked twenty years younger. She wore a very trim, pale-pink suit and had her hair piled high in a bouffant style. Fashionable spectacles and well-applied make-up completed the picture. In the eighties we were not as used to world travel as we are now, and Evelyn came over as being very different, as being very, very American. But when she spoke, she spoke right to our hearts.

It was with a sense of expectation that I introduced her. And, had I thought about it, I would have been even more amazed at my standing addressing 650 women than about her coming half way across the world to speak to us. I just didn't do things like that!

Evelyn's teaching was simple. It was basic. But it seemed so fresh and new. Having discussed the power of prayer, those things which hinder prayer and our need to pray in one accord, she based the remainder of her morning seminar on six S's.

Firstly, we learned to pray *subject by subject*. When praying as part of a group, she suggested that we should not each go through long lists of prayer topics, just in case anyone or anything was left out. Instead, subjects should be given out one at a time, thus allowing everyone to focus on each subject and take it together to the Lord. How often when we pray with others, our 'amen' at the end of their prayers is not 100 per cent, for instead of listening and praying with them, we are thinking ahead to what we want to pray for when they stop speaking. Now why had I not thought of that?

Secondly, she suggested that we should keep our prayers *short and to the point*. For many of the women gathered there that day, praying aloud with others would be a new experience. Some came from Christian traditions in which only men led in prayer, and often at length. The thought of having to compose a long prayer could have been a very daunting prospect to someone who was new to it. Evelyn taught us to pray on single subjects, and in only one or two sentences. Even the shyest member of a prayer group could learn to contribute in that way.

Her third point was that we should pray *simply*. Most of those present that day came from backgrounds where 'to lead in prayer' meant following a pattern and using words and phrases which were almost the technical language of prayer. Why was that necessary, she challenged us; does God not understand simple language? We knew he did.

Evelyn told us that we should be *specific* in our praying, making specific requests and giving thanks for specific answers. When I thought over my own prayer life I knew I often poured out so many intercessions to the Lord that I would hardly have noticed if one was answered. And, having prayed, I felt I had done my duty, forgetting that I should be looking expectantly for God's answer in order to thank him for it. How many children, having asked their parent for something, would then wander off without waiting for an answer?

Fifthly, she advocated *times of silence* between prayers. As she spoke I smiled to myself, I knew just what she was going to say. Hadn't I often prayed just to fill a silence? Now I was reminded that prayer is a two-way conversation. We speak to God and we should leave time and space and silence to allow him to speak to us.

And lastly, Evelyn recommended that we pray in *small groups*. We had become used to thinking that Americans believed that 'big is beautiful', but here we were being told that in prayer the opposite is true. I knew I found large groups inhibiting because by nature I am shy. For anyone with a hearing impairment a large prayer group must be a very isolating experience. Yes, I could think of several reasons for meeting in small groups, not least the ability to share more confidentially regarding matters for prayer.

Our speaker, having gone through the mechanics of praying, set us to prayer. In effect, we practised praying. We broke into groups and prayed: short, specific, single subject prayers, using simple language with periods of silence between the topics. It felt strange. It was so different from what we were used to. But we could do it. Many women prayed aloud in company for the first time. There was a feeling of release. We were beginning to discover what happens when women pray. And the first thing we discovered was that we had a new freedom.

Annette chaired the afternoon session and I sat with Wilma in the front of the balcony. It was with a sense of wonder that I looked round the hundreds of women present. Surely, I concluded, God had brought us together for a reason. Was today the reason, what plans did he have in store for us? Evelyn began speaking and I was immediately caught up in the truths of which she spoke.

'What do you mean,' she challenged us, 'when you pray for God's will to be done?' I knew that it was sometimes used as a 'cop out', allowing me to feel that if God did not seem to have answered a prayer then it was because it was not his will. Now it seemed that prayer was the submitting of our wills to God. How often I had tried to force my will on him. I was going to have to do some serious thinking.

Evelyn talked about commitment in prayer. I was glad about that for I wanted the women to hear what she was saying. It was not that I thought I knew it all, rather I wanted them to avoid the hurts to which I had subjected myself during my early married life when I had treated God like the fourth emergency service, calling on him in much the same way as I would have called the police, an ambulance or the fire brigade, only in a crisis. But what she said applied to me too. I resolved to be more committed in my prayer life.

It was a relief after dealing with the strong subject of commitment when our speaker turned to upholstery and told us about her old green chair. Her audience relaxed as it listened. Evelyn's green chair was where she prayed, she explained, going on to stress the importance of a specific place of prayer. Of course we pray in different places, in churches, meeting halls, hospitals and homes. But the private place of prayer has to be thought about rather than stumbled upon. I did not know it then but before very long I was to discover that God had a place of prayer all mapped out for me.

'To whom do you pray?' Evelyn asked. Well, I thought, we all knew the answer to that. But I doubt I had realised its implications. If we were praying to the God of gods and King of kings, could we really barge into his presence without considering who we were daring to approach? Wise woman that she was, she also warned us that Satan was prowling around looking for company, and that if we did not focus on the Lord, the devil would try to divert us and, yes, he would listen to our prayers and answer them according to his evil purposes. That was a new thought and a disturbing one.

Wondering how much more I could take in, I listened on. After the warning about Satan it was reassuring to consider the results of prayer. We probably all knew something of the unifying effects of prayer, even over great distances. I already had experience of incidents where missionaries were supported through difficult times, only to discover afterwards that the Lord had laid it on the hearts of some of their friends to pray for them at exactly their time of need.

And having discussed the vertical nature of prayer – communication between believers and God, and God and his children – Evelyn turned to the horizontal. Reminding us of the Lord's words as he taught his disciples to pray, 'Forgive us our debts, as we also have forgiven our debtors' (Matt. 6:12), she stressed the need for forgiveness. Just a moment's reflection made me realise this was yet another subject to which I would have to apply myself. I was struggling with forgiveness. What a lot there was to take in!

Evelyn drew to a close by telling us about telephone prayer chains. She explained that these were made up of people who were committed to prayer and that a system was set up whereby they could be called to pray when needs arose. Although this was in **What Happens When Women Pray?** I had not really taken in the practicalities of how it worked. I listened on as she gave examples from her own experience of how God had used the Prayer Chain Ministry.

With that Evelyn closed, but not before she had invited any who were interested in being part of a prayer chain for the nation to place their badges bearing their names, addresses and telephone numbers in a box at the door as they left. Wilma and I looked at each other. We looked down at Annette who was staring up in our direction. But we couldn't see clearly through the tears in our eyes. We knew, all three of us knew without a shadow of doubt, that this was God's answer to our prayers. This was how he was going to encourage prayer for our sad and sick nation. We were overwhelmed by the vastness of it all. And we wept.

Women had travelled from Inverness, Aberdeen, the Borders and all over the central belt of Scotland. As they left to catch their trains and buses, 450 of them put their badges into the box. When we counted them later we were thrilled, humbled too but really thrilled that 450 women in Scotland had been challenged by the teaching they had heard from Evelyn and wanted to apply it by committing themselves to prayer. We are used to small beginnings. This was no small beginning, it was a huge one. But there was a long, long way to go. God's wonderful plan was set in motion and we stood in awe at what he had done.

6

Prayer Chain Ministry

More things are wrought by prayer
Than this world dreams of.
(Alfred, Lord Tennyson)

To have 450 women willing to commit themselves to prayer for the nation was one thing, to organise them into doing that in an informed way was quite another, BUT GOD knew the plans he had in store. Annette took on the task of creating the prayer chain. Dividing the country into areas, she found a group leader for each area. The women were then divided between the group leaders. This allowed for the operation of the chain. To pass on items for prayer, all Annette had to do was phone one group leader plus the first person in her own group. The group leader she contacted would phone the first person on her own chain and the next group leader. Within a year, a thousand women were members. It became necessary to appoint regional leaders with group leaders under them, but the chain effect worked in the same way, there were just more links in it.

A few months later, Annette told me the news that she and her husband were moving to Switzerland.

'You'll take over as leader of Prayer Chain,' she concluded. 'No, not me,' I was adamant, 'I'm not a leader.' Placing her hand on my shoulder she opened her Bible and read, 'The angel of the LORD gave this charge to Joshua: "This is what the LORD Almighty says: 'If you will walk in my ways and keep my requirements, then you will govern my house and have charge of my courts, and I will give you a place among these standing here'"' (Zech. 3:6-7). I did take over as leader but I struggled – how I struggled. And I was still struggling in 1983 when Evelyn Christenson came back to do another seminar. One of the exercises we did that day involved going through Romans 12 and writing a letter to ourselves based on the chapter. The struggle was over. God spoke to me through part of verse 8: if a man's gift is 'leadership, let him govern diligently'. And Peter, who had said 'No' to any suggestion of my taking on a job, backed me wholeheartedly. This was God's work.

The prayer requests were telephoned out on Monday evenings at 6pm, and the women committed themselves to being by their phones to receive the calls. The domino effect was such that within two hours all 1,000 women were called to prayer. From time to time we received emergency calls and these were sent out as they came in. The number which was given for prayer requests was our phone number. Peter was very patient about it, but I have to admit it did dominate our lives. Calls came at every time of day ... and night. Meals were interrupted, jobs abandoned, television programmes unfinished, and our kitchen table? It is a subject all on its own!

Evelyn Christenson's green chair was her place of prayer. My kitchen table was mine. But it was more than that, it was my office too. It was at it that I noted requests as they came in. It was there I spread all my papers as I made up the weekly prayer lists. This took a bit of organising as only some topics went to all the groups. Others, which were personal or of more local interest, only went to the region or regions to which they most applied. And it was there too that I spent many long hours writing letters.

As God had burdened my heart for the nation, now he opened my eyes more and more to what was happening around me. I realised that to act without praying was a futile exercise, but to pray without acting was not enough.

Looking back over the last fifty years we can see the insidious way in which Christian standards have been eroded by the media. Eminent churchmen on radio and television have encouraged Christians to accept humanist views, rejecting the existence of God and ridiculing fundamental doctrines of the Christian faith. This reached a climax in the Sixties when the headlines read, '"God is dead," says bishop'. And the media has promoted immorality to such a degree that Christian marriage and family life are now seen as quaint hangovers from former times. Even children's story books are in on the act, some going as far as featuring homosexual relationships in order to show that there is nothing wrong with 'alternative lifestyles'.

Also in the Sixties blasphemy, foul language, sex and violence entered the nation's living rooms through its television sets. Although I saw this happening I, like many others, stood back and let the floodgates open. Someone has said that, 'Evil triumphs when good men do nothing.' Mary Whitehouse, who was often the butt of media jokes, stood almost alone, fighting on our behalf. How much we owe to her courage and tenacity.

It was some time before I realised that if I was earnest in my prayers for decency on BBC and ITV, surely I should write complimenting them when they did produce good material and pointing out to them when they did not. My burden for the government drove me to write dozens of letters to Members of Parliament. And the piles on my kitchen table grew. I am convinced that if Christians take up their pens, remembering that one with God is a majority, we would become a force mighty under God in the pushing back of evil rather than the silent minority we often are. When we hear the name of our great God blasphemed on radio or television it should grieve our hearts and inspire us to write. If Mohammed's name was so abused there would be a holy war!

About this time Peter and I read *The Trumpet Sounds for Britain* by David E Gardner. It seemed to reflect exactly our assessment of the state of the United Kingdom. Gardner compared the country's plight to that of a great ship on a collision course with icebergs, and with her radio and radar switched off. Ignoring all warnings, passing all danger signals, she steams on towards a disaster of titanic proportions. We bought three-dozen copies of the book and sent it to leaders in politics, industry, the church and the media. Many thanked us for the book. It was our prayer that it would be read and would speak to those who had received it.

Prayer Chain at that time concentrated more, although not exclusively, on the needs of individuals. It is interesting to look back over the years at the topics for prayer that were sent out and how they have changed over the years. At the beginning of 1982, for example, the list looked like this:

All groups: Pray for Mary Whitehouse and those who fight a lone battle against evil.

Group 3: Pray for a young man who is involved in perverted sexual practices. His parents and other relatives want us to pray for his release from this evil and for his salvation.

All groups: British Telecom has introduced Dial-a-Horoscope. Pray that this may be stopped.

Group 6: Pray for M, aged 8, who has a genetic condition. Pray for his healing and that his parents' faith may be strengthened.

Group 2: Christian Literature Crusade – pray for their speaker who is giving a talk on morality in a school this week.

Having made these calls to prayer, the topics were followed up and a bi-monthly bulletin produced telling how the Lord had answered. It warms my soul to read over back issues. And I have no doubt that the following excerpts were both a source of praise and a spur to prayer.

Remember L, paralyzed with a virus, that the Lord would heal her and grant her plenty to occupy her mind.

She's on her feet and back to work, but needs prayer with coping.

Pray for A's sister-in-law, that she might come to know the Lord.

Trusted in God, and doing really well. Her husband trusted the Lord as well.

Pray for the distributors and recipients of 20,000 copies of Good News Gospel of John being distributed in the Falkirk area in the next three weeks. Pray that they will be read and that the Holy Spirit may work in the hearts of those who receive them.

Gospels well received. Many attended the meetings.

Not all our prayers were answered in the way we would have chosen. We were often reminded of the sovereignty of God. That same bulletin records one such occasion.

Pray for R in intensive care following surgery.

R progressed well, was moved back to the ward and seemed to be making excellent progress. He had a relapse and died suddenly.

There was no question of us thinking that when 1,000 women gathered with one request we could manipulate God, that there was somehow power in our number. Far from it. We saw our praying as drawing together with God, and working alongside him towards the fulfilment of his purposes. Paul calls us God's fellow workers (2 Cor. 6:1). When we brought our prayers to the Lord, we brought them in the spirit of handing them to him, knowing that his will is best in every situation.

Many of us never outgrow a childish concept of prayer and continue to see it as 'God bless me and mine, thee and thine; us four and no more', though we dress it in sophisticated language! The more I learned about prayer the more exciting the whole idea became, and the more I enjoyed my times of prayer. Sadly, that does not mean that I find it easy to pray, because the very act of getting to prayer must be one of the areas in my life in which the devil is most active, and most effective. He places all sorts of barriers in the way of prayer, and it takes concentrated effort to push them to the side. It has been said that important things are left undone because urgent things take up our time. There can be no area in our lives of which that is truer than prayer.

Intercession is a lonely business, and there may be days or even years when there appears to be no answer. Peter and I have been praying for members of our family for many years. We can get discouraged, but in Matthew 22:22 Jesus encourages us to pray believing that we will receive an answer. Perseverance takes courage and determination. It is said that 301 banks rejected Walt Disney's request for a loan before he finally got one, but because he refused to quit he built the world's most famous theme park. Our Lord faced more discouragement than we can ever know. Imagine if on his way to the cross, he suddenly cried out to his Father. 'I've had enough, I can't do this, I quit!' Where would we be? But thank God he went all the way to Calvary.

A father, trying to encourage his son in his academic studies said, 'You must never quit when things get tough. Look at David Livingstone, did he quit when things got tough? What about Edison, did he quit? What about the Wright brothers and what about Jonathan McPringle?' 'Who is Jonanthan McPringle?' asked his son. 'I've never heard of him.' 'Of course not,' said his father, 'because he quit.'

We know that if our hearts are right with God he will answer in his time and in his way.

Oswald Chambers said that 'Prayer is the highest order or business for God, for it links a powerless human to the creative forces of God's sovereign power.' Daniel was a man who did business for God and knew the power of God in his life. Daniel expresses the reality of God in these words. '[T]he people who know their God shall be strong and do exploits and they that understand among the people shall instruct many' (Dan. 11:32, KJV). Daniel was raised to fulfil God's purposes. He lived his life in an attitude of prayer. It has been said that 'Knowing God leads to experiencing his power. Yielding my entire life to that power sets in motion the purposes of God in my life and *my Church.*' (emphasis added).

We were made to know God. '[T]his is eternal life, that they may know you, the only true God, and Jesus Christ, whom you have sent' (John 17:3). How can we find real joy, and contentment other than by knowing God? 'This is what the LORD says: Let not the wise man boast of his wisdom or the strong man boast of his strength or the rich man boast of his riches, but let him boasts boast about this: that he understands and knows me, that I am the LORD, who exercises kindness, justice and righteousness on earth, for in these I delight' (Jer. 9:23-4).

J.I. Packer has written in his book *The Christian Life and how to Live It* 'now that you have come to know God, or rather to be known by God....' (Gal. 4:9, NASB). What comes to the surface in this qualifying clause is the apostle's sense that grace came first, and remains fundamental, in his reader's salvation. Their knowledge of God was the consequence of God's taking knowledge of them. They know him by faith because he first singled them out by grace.

> Know! When used of God in this way, is a sovereign-grace word, pointing to God's initiative in loving, choosing, redeeming, calling and preserving. That God is fully aware of us, 'knowing us through and through' as we say, is certainly part of what is meant, as appears from the imperfect knowledge of God and his perfect knowledge of us in 1 Corinthians 13:12.... What matters supremely, is not, in the last analysis, the fact that I know God, but the larger fact which underlies it – the fact that he *knows me*. I am graven on the palms of his hands. I am never out of his mind. All my knowledge of him depends on his sustained initiative in knowing me. I know him, because he first knew me, and continues to know me. He knows me as a friend, one who loves me, and there is no moment when his eye is off me, or his attention is distracted from me, and no moment, therefore when his care falters.

WOW!

As I have already said I love the expression, 'nothing takes God by surprise', He knows all the circumstances that make up my problems, my concerns, my worries, and he knows the solutions, but he holds back until prayer is made from earth. I must confess I do not understand why the Almighty God of the universe wants me to pray. He certainly doesn't need me to pray, but when he hears a prayer from the heart of someone who is captive to his will, he responds. God may achieve this by arranging circumstances, which cause us to be burdened about someone or something, and so we give ourselves to pray. This was the situation when Nebuchadnezzar had a dream (Dan. 2).

When the king called for his wise men and astrologers to interpret the dream, they could not reveal it, and he ordered them to be executed. Daniel went to the king and asked for time to interpret the dream. Did Daniel run to his friends for their advice? No, he asked them to a prayer meeting and explained the situation. God gave Daniel the interpretation of the king's dream, and the key to defuse the destructive decree. Nebuchadnezzar was made to realize that the message of the dream was from Almighty God who is the King of kings and God of gods. So he appointed Daniel, God's man, to be ruler of the province of Babylon, and Babylon's political structure was changed.

Arthur Wallace, in his book *Born for Battle*, explains the 'cutting edge of prayer'. 'Prayer is the cutting edge of any work for God. It is not a supplemental spiritual rocket to get some well-meaning effort off the ground. Prayer is the work and the working power in any spiritual ministry. It should be the central thrust. The spiritual history of a mission or a Church is written in its prayer life. The expression of corporate life is not measured in statistics, but in prayer depth. The program of preaching, teaching and serving, the goal setting, the adoption of new techniques, seminars on time management and administrative procedures are all good, but effective and productive in God's economy as they are subject to prayer ... And so in all the work for God, prayer is the working power of all that God would do through His people. Without waiting on God for Him to reveal His will, our well-meant attemptings may look impressive, but they have no power to move towards God's goal.'

I am old enough to look back and remember 'old fashioned prayer meetings' (whatever happened to them?), and the power and excitement of meeting with God. The spiritual power of the church depended on its prayer life. People were added to the church by being saved, not by being recycled! Men and women who had been rescued from the pit of hell touched the Throne of God, and all could feel the power of the Holy Spirit. Hearts were stoked with the fire of God and we prayed because the Holy Spirit drew us to pray. Over the years I have witnessed reality disappearing and prayer meetings becoming boring, prayers becoming stale repetitions and often in the same words.

A Spirit-filled, Spirit-controlled, Spirit-anointed church will be a praying church. Where he is not grieved he will always be engaging the church in a movement of prayer, but where there is a wrong attitude, criticism or a bad spirit, there is no freedom to pray in the Spirit. We can know all the doctrines about prayer but that doesn't mean that our hearts have been set on fire to pray by the Spirit of God. We pray because God's Spirit draws us to pray; only he gives that thirst. We pray because the power of God is released through prayer.

I thank God for the Scottish Christian Youth Rallies where, in the early 1950s, young men and women came together for a Converts' Class on a Wednesday evening and for a prayer meeting each Friday. We met in the Christian Institute in Bothwell Street, Glasgow where for three hours we knelt on the floor with our elbows on our chairs and poured out our hearts to God, often with tears and brokenness. God's love for us and our love for him melted our hearts. We pleaded for the souls of men and women; we stood in the gap for those in trouble and for many family concerns. In so doing, we learned to pray and open ourselves to God and his Holy Spirit.

A student of the subject of prayer will be rewarded with great treasures. What more amazing fact can there be than that God wants us to pray; the Creator and Sustainer of the entire universe wants you and me to talk to him! Jesus, God's Son, who prayed himself, also taught his followers to pray. And not only does God want us to speak to him, he hears and answers us. 'Praise awaits you, O God, in Zion; to you our vows will be fulfilled. O you who hear prayer, to you all men will come... You answer us with awesome deeds of righteousness, O God our Saviour, the hope of all the ends of the earth and of the farthest seas, who formed the mountains by your power, having armed yourself with strength, who stilled the roaring of the seas, the roaring of their waves, and the turmoil of the nations' (Ps. 65:1-2, 5-7). The God who did all those things wants to hear and answer my prayers!

Prayer is also a great release. 'Do not be anxious about anything, but in everything, by prayer and petition, with thanksgiving, present your requests to God. And the peace of God, which transcends all understanding, will guard your hearts and your minds in Christ Jesus' (Phil. 4:6-7). How often we forfeit our peace through lack of prayer. In an unholy effort at independence we carry our burdens alone, allowing anxieties to become big worries that attack our hearts and minds, making us heavy-hearted and depressed. God, who created us and understands us, offers to protect the areas in which we are most vulnerable. Prayer protects our hearts and minds.

Corrie Ten Boom relates this story in her book *Jesus is Victor*. Corrie was invited to be the guest speaker at a Japanese Church in Tokyo. In the light of the horror the people had suffered as a result of the atomic bomb, when two of their greatest cities had been destroyed, she wondered what she could say to them. So she decided to give them an object lesson. 'Do you know the feeling,' she began, 'when your heart is like a suitcase with a heavy load?' She told them that she was weary from tramping around the world carrying her heavy suitcase, but God had given her a glorious verse in the Bible which says, 'Cast all your anxieties on him for he cares about you.' To illustrate her talk, she filled a case with various small packages, and spoke of all the problems we often carry. 'Lord', she said, 'Here are my co-workers. They are so tired.' She reached down and took two items out of the suitcase and laid them on the table. She continued bringing family, friends and situations to the Lord, and each time bringing an object out of her suitcase and laying it on the table. In the end the suitcase was empty and she closed it and pretended to walk out of the room swinging her light bag as though it was made of paper. The people immediately got her point. After the meeting she quickly threw all the items back into her suitcase and left to join her hosts.

A number of years later Corrie was in Berlin at an international congress on evangelism when a distinguished-looking Japanese gentleman approached her. 'Corrie Ten Boom,' he said with a broad smile, 'every time I hear your name I think of your trouble suitcase.'

'Oh,' she said, flattered, 'I'm so glad you remembered what I said that night.'

'It was not what you said that I remember', he smiled, 'It was what you did.'

'You remember me taking all those objects out of my suitcase and laying them on the table as an illustration of how to pray?'

'No, that is not what I remember most,' he said. 'What I remember most is that after you finished your talk, you took all the objects, put them back in your suitcase and walked out of the hall just as burdened as when you came in.'

I can associate with this, as I often do the same thing – pray and ask God to take the burdens, and then after a few minutes I take them all back again. I have found a way to help me in this. I take an object, like a book, and when I pray for an issue, I deliberately place the book down and say, 'Lord this is my burden and I'm giving it to you.' I may have to do this many times before I know that I have relinquished my burden to the Lord.

There is more to prayer than speaking to God each morning and evening. 'Be joyful always; pray continually; give thanks in all circumstances, for this is God's will for you in Christ Jesus' (1 Thess. 5:16-18). As well as praying prayers, God asks us to live in an attitude of prayer all the time. We do that by sharpening our awareness of his presence, by taking joys and sorrows, thanks and needs to him as the day goes on rather than saving them up till bedtime.

Brother Lawrence, a sixteenth-century monk who spent his time cleaning in a monastery, practised the presence of God while doing his daily chores. He did not find life easy in the monastery. There were some mean-spirited monks who were jealous of his sanctity and they made his life a misery. They found imaginary spots on his pans and made him wash them again; they spilled things on the floor and made him scrub it again; they campaigned to humiliate and break him. But Brother Lawrence prayed for his fellow monks, thanking God for them. He saw them as God's instruments to refine and purify his life. He would not go to sleep with hard thoughts of them on his heart. He believed that this persecution and suffering must come with God's permission, if not his will, and if that was so he could bring great gain if rightly used. So he poured himself into the extra work, the shame and humiliation and offered not resentment, but love. In the end those who had so ill-used him realized they were not fit to touch his sandals. But he thought of them as friends, sent from God to refine and make him more like his Lord.

It is especially important to cultivate the practice of asking God's forgiveness as soon as we realise we have sinned. We say 'sorry' right away in human relationships, so isn't it strange that we collect our sins into a bundle before bringing them to God for forgiveness?

We are not alone in our prayers. The Bible tells us that as we are praying for others our Saviour is praying for us. 'Christ Jesus, who died – more than that, who was raised to life – is at the right hand of God and is also interceding for us' (Rom. 8:34). Scripture gives us a glimpse of ourselves in glory. 'Dear friends, now we are children of God, and what we will be has not yet been made known. But we know that when he appears, we shall be like him, for we shall see him as he is' (1 John 3:2). Christ is prayerful. He is our Great High Priest, who is ever interceding for us, 'because Jesus lives for ever, he has a permanent priesthood. Therefore he is able to save completely those who come to God through him, because he always lives to intercede for them' (Heb. 7:24, 25). In our prayerfulness we become more like him. As we grow to be like the people we spend time with, it is little wonder that Satan is determined to distract us from having close fellowship with our God. One of the blessings of Prayer Chain is the discipline it involves. It is less easy to let prayer lapse if we have our minds concentrated and our diaries organised to allow for it.

Probably many of the women involved would have been content for us to have an intercessory ministry for those with special needs, for needs there were aplenty. But the vision Wilma, Annette and I had was of a nation in need of prayer and 1,000 women praying for the nation. By 1986 the focus was beginning to move in that direction, as these snippets from the August and September prayer lists show.

> Continued prayer is needed for the fight for the protection of the unborn child. Urge your MP to support the Ten Minute Rule Bill being introduced on 21st October.

> Pray for young people returning to school and for the education system, that it will meet their needs spiritually and morally as well as educationally.

> A department store in Norfolk has engaged a clairvoyant to provide a free fortune-telling service for shoppers. Pray against this project.

> Channel 4 is considering a special magazine for gays; now the BBC is planning to introduce a gay couple into a soap opera. Pray.

> The Focus Trust is producing a film of William Tyndale and it is likely that Channel 4 will agree to screen it. Pray for its production, the necessary finances, and that Channel 4 will accept it.

> A woman calling herself a white witch is active in the Helensburgh Area. Pray that Christians will be victorious in that setting and that wrong will be overcome.

In 1981 I had put a prayer through the newly formed prayer chain asking God to introduce us to a man who was educated in politics and who would advise us how to pray for our nation. Yet again, he knew the plans he had for us.

7

Within the walls of Westminster

And Satan trembles when he sees
The weakest saint upon his knees.
(William Cowper)

We need a little history lesson before we can go on. Shortly after General Eisenhower became President of the United States of America, he confided in one of his Senators, Frank Carlson, that he had had a wartime experience of God. Carlson understood. He too met God on a battlefield. They talked about their faith. In the course of the conversation, President Eisenhower told Carlson that being President was the loneliest job he had ever done and that the White House was the loneliest house he had lived in. Frank Carlson invited President Eisenhower to join a group of Senators in a prayer breakfast. The result was the establishment of the Washington Prayer Breakfast, now held every February and hosted by the President. The thousands of people who attend are encouraged to pray for their nation.

In 1984, what was the First London Prayer Breakfast, which later became The Parliamentary Prayer Breakfast, was held. We were invited to attend through our friends John and Louise Purvis. Louise was a co-founder of Prison Fellowship here in Scotland. John was an EEC Member of Parliament. It was quite an experience! Five hundred people met at 7.30am in London's Savoy Hotel. After we were welcomed the following statement of purpose was read.

Since 1661 the Parliamentary day has started with this prayer:

Almighty God, by whom alone Kings reign, and princes decree justice; and from whom alone cometh all counsel, wisdom, and understanding; We, thine unworthy servants, here gathered together in thy Name, do most humbly beseech thee to send down thy Heavenly Wisdom from above, to direct and guide us in all our consultations: And grant that, we having thy fear always before our eyes, and laying aside all private interests, prejudices, and partial affections, the result of all our counsels may be to the glory of thy blessed name, the maintenance of true Religion and Justice, the safety, honour, and happiness of the queen, the public wealth, peace, and tranquillity of the realm, and the uniting and knitting together of the hearts of all persons and estates within the same, in true Christian love and Charity one towards another, through Jesus Christ our Lord and Saviour. Amen.

In this spirit, members of the Parliamentary Christian Fellowship, which meets to deepen friendships, to pray and take counsel together, inaugurated the National Prayer Breakfast specifically to seek God's guidance and strength and to renew the dedication of our nation and ourselves to him and his purposes. This event in our capital city seeks to encourage men and women throughout the United Kingdom and the world to recognise their privileges and responsibilities before God.

Our desire is that leaders at all levels of society should be enabled by God to strengthen the spiritual life and moral values of the nation, and that many of them will meet back in their own locality in the same spirit of Jesus Christ, bridging party, social and economic differences. As a natural outgrowth of gatherings such as this, people in many parts of the world are finding, through the power of Jesus Christ, a fellowship that is helping to build true community in the family of nations.

It thrilled my soul. Having been burdened by the state of the United Kingdom I was overwhelmed to find so many people ardent in their prayers for it, for our government and for our future.

After breakfast, Bishop Bill Burnet spoke on, 'if my people, who are called by my name, will humble themselves and pray and seek my face and turn from their wicked ways, then will I hear from heaven and will forgive their sin and will heal their land' (2 Chron. 7:14). His was no academic discourse. It was full of down-to-earth practicalities. Having preached humility, he warned us of the devil's trick of making us proud of being humble. Bishop Burnet's illustration hit home and stuck. He was breakfasting with his wife one day when their waitress, seeing his bishop's clerical colours, asked, 'And what kind of holy man are you, Robin Redbreast?' Her banter made him think and led to him having a new experience of God. But after just three days of being humbled by it he realised that he was beginning to feel proud of being humble. That was not the kind of humility God required from our nation. His demands are taxing, but the rewards last to eternity.

That Prayer Breakfast was thrilling, but even *it* was not without its little problems. Peter and I met there something we had not done before. After each speaker concluded his message, those present applauded. They clapped! Now that really made us feel uncomfortable. It seemed as though we were praising the speaker rather than the God of whom he spoke. But reflection showed us otherwise. This was not razzmatazz. The mood of the meeting was reverent, even holy, and the sense of the Lord was very real. Our applause was tentative and embarrassed but we began to realise that they were clapping not the speakers but the Lord. Although it took me quite a time to feel uninhibited in my applause of God, I now wonder why.

That morning, God answered our prayer for a man educated in politics when Peter and I were introduced to Anthony Cordle. And if anyone knew what was going on inside the Palace of Westminster, Anthony did. His was a unique ministry there. Although he was not a Member of Parliament, he had passes to both the Lords and the Commons where he drew alongside Members in a chaplaincy role, encouraging believers and befriending others. He had contacts in all parties and at every level. I shared my vision of Prayer Chain being committed to praying for the nation in an intelligent and informed way. And when the Cordles visited us in Scotland a short time later I told him of Prayer Chain's petition that God would lead us to someone who would be able to direct our prayers for the nation. He agreed to help us find someone suitable. Patricia Park became our first Parliamentary contact. Miles, her husband, was one of those who initiated the London Prayer Breakfast. Little did I know then how important that introduction to Patricia and Miles was to be. God was setting the stage, arranging the characters in the next chapter of my adventure with him. And Prayer Chain took another step forward.

Snatches from the diary give an indication of the information we received.

Praise the Lord for the debate on the Warnock Report. Out of twenty-five speakers there were eighteen pro-life or Christian. Another debate will be held in the House of Commons. Pray that many pro-life and Christian Members of Parliament will speak out strongly against those things which violate God's laws.

20.12.84 – Heard from parliamentary contact that a bomb is to go off some time over the Christmas period in London. Pray that it will be found and safely defused.

3.1.85 – Praise the Lord! The London bomb was found.

7.1.85 – Enoch Powell is sponsoring the Second Reading of the Warnock Bill on 15.2.85. Pray that hundreds of MPs will be present and vote in favour of The Unborn Children Protection Bill. Pray that the Government will make time available for all the Committee Stage proceedings.

15.1.85 – Some MPs are planning to block Mr Powell's Private Member's Bill. A meeting to co-ordinate opposition is being held today. Pray. Members of the House of Commons, House of Lords and the press meet today at 11am to be briefed by eminent authorities on artificial insemination and in-vitro fertilization. Pray that those lecturing may be given wisdom.

5.3.85 Enoch Powell's Bill has been given early committee time on Wednesday. Pray that the chairman, David Knox, will be favourable to the Bill. There is to be a house party of 38 MPs and their wives this weekend. John Stott is the speaker. Pray for six non-Christian MPs who will be present.

19.3.85 – Praise the Lord! The house party was a spiritual success. The feedback is very positive.

26.3.85 – Mr Powell's Bill will reach the Report Stage on 3rd May. Pray. Write to your MP encouraging him to be present as it is the holiday weekend.

27.11.85 – Lord Brentford, Chairman of a group trying to get an amendment to the Sunday Trading Bill through the House of Lords, is meeting Mr Whitelaw today and Douglas Hurd tomorrow. Pray for God's will to be done. Pray that the eight peers invited to vote on Tuesday will turn up and give a majority vote for the amendment. Pray daily till Tuesday.

A Bill to strengthen the 1959 Obscene Publications Act by including a much tighter definition of obscenity has won sixth place in a ballot for Commons time. Pray about this.

Mr. Winston Churchill is to introduce a Bill to the House of Commons against sadistic violence on video films. Pray.

Such was the developing interest in, and commitment to, praying for the nation that people began to question when national issues did not feature on our weekly prayer lists. One member put it well. 'I go to our (church) prayer meeting and sit and listen to our prayers for me, mine and thine and I want to stand up, hold out my Prayer Chain notebook, and shout, "Look at the things you can be praying for in the nation!"'

In order to encourage the women in prayer, the Regional Leaders organised regular, usually monthly, meetings. This helped them to solve difficulties before they became big problems and to share their concerns. It also stimulated them to pray for each other. I tried to visit as many groups as I could, especially those in more remote areas. It was a real joy meeting with women from varying backgrounds, and being encouraged by their enthusiasm as they looked forward each week to the issues for prayer.

Prayer Chain had changed my life and even more changes were afoot. Coming from a Christian Brethren background I did not naturally think of women in the role of speakers. It therefore came as a real surprise to find myself cast in that role. For years I had been happy to give demonstrations at ladies meetings. I might have been known as the 'lampshade lady' for all I know, having demonstrated the making of so many of them.

But that was not 'speaking'. I had sung in public since my earliest days and had no qualms about sharing the gospel in song. But that was not 'speaking'. Speaking was for Peter, not for me. When a missionary friend invited me, twenty-four years ago, to go with her to Ireland for a week and to sing at several meetings she was addressing I readily agreed. When, as we crossed on the ferry, she told me she believed God was calling me to speak to women I was gobsmacked. But she was serious. And at one meeting she, without prior warning, asked me to share a little about Peter's prison ministry. I did speak and what a mess I made of it. That, I thought, was the beginning and the end of my career as a public speaker. But my friend pursued the subject on the return journey. I laughed, the thought of that embarrassing meeting still fresh in my mind. 'I'll pray about it,' she concluded. And if ever there was a conversation stopper that was it! Discussing it later with Peter I was challenged by his wry observation, 'How is it that you can demonstrate lampshade making but you can't speak about the Lord?' Flower arranging and lampshade making were my natural gifts, but through my demonstrations God was preparing me to use my spiritual gifts, gifts of which I was not even aware. I had been comfortable giving my practical demonstrations and the devil would have kept me doing them, so distracting me from God's best gifts – getting to know him through prayer and helping others to do the same.

Looking through my 1985 diary I find it full of engagements: singing solos, ladies choir, and ... yes ... speaking. I must have worn down the roads of the central belt of Scotland as I drove to meetings, sometimes three or four in a week. But one engagement in 1985 stands out. I was invited to be one of the speakers, along with Baroness Cox, at the seminar following the Second London Prayer Breakfast, which was now called the Parliamentary Prayer Breakfast as it was hosted by parliamentarians. In 1985 the host was Lord Tonypandy, Speaker of the House of Commons. My response when asked was an incredulous 'Who? Me?' And it felt like 'Who? Me?' on the day. I had the most amazing experience as I spoke, as though I was standing outside my own body listening to someone else speaking. Had I been there in my own strength I should have crumpled into a quivering heap behind the podium. **But God's** was the strength and he spoke and touched several lives.

On returning home to Scotland I contacted my friend Annie Black, from whom I had asked prayer support. 'Do you know what I prayed?' she asked. 'I prayed that God would shut you up and that he would speak.' How wise she was. And God heard and answered her prayer. It was my experience then, and it has been over and again since as I have addressed groups and conferences, that God has given me praying friends who have upheld me through my times of preparation, my speaking engagements and the days of tiredness that follow them. I wonder if secretaries who write inviting speakers to come to their meetings realise that they are calling their speakers' prayer supporters to participate too.

8

A lesson in obedience

But Thou are good, and goodness still
delighteth to forgive.
(Robert Burns)

Prayer Chain fought spiritual battles and won. But it also fought spiritual battles and lost. And from time to time it fought on the enemy's side by disobeying the commands of our Great Captain. There follows an account of such an engagement. It gives me no pleasure to tell of it, **but God** in his goodness redeems situations as well as souls and I believe that we withdrew from our defeat only to be stronger in his service.

In our spiritual battles we can fight on three battlefields: the world, the flesh and the devil. And we need to determine in which field our particular battle is being fought. So many times when we blame Satan the problem is in our own flesh. We surrender to anxiety rather than trusting, we worry rather than obey. Our battlefield on this occasion was the flesh, manifested in an unholy independence and lack of trust.

George Müller's life of faith and trust in God made an impact on my life as a young woman. He was responsible for the care of thousands of orphan children in mid nineteenth-century Bristol and trusted God to meet all their needs. So early in the administration of Prayer Chain, I made a promise to the Lord that we would not ask for money, but make the need known only to him.

I wrote what follows on the 19th January 1984.

'Prayer Chain Ministry is an organism which God, by his Spirit, initiated on September 1981, the original vision being 'national prayer for Scotland'.

In the early months of this ministry the Lord led me to the book of Ezra to learn lessons, the chief one being, why the vision to pray for our nation was not being totally fulfilled.

a. Ezra 4:4 explained the inevitable discouragements and Satan's activity when God is at work.

b. Ezra 3:11-12 showed that not everyone was prepared to accept this 'new thing' and break from tradition.

c. Ezra 6:8 assured us that the expenses would be met from God's Royal Treasury so that the work will not stop.

d. Showed us the need for confession and repentance before God could use us with effect (Ps. 66:18).

In October 1983 P.C.M. asked 'For what purpose has God united 1000 praying women from every denomination in Scotland?'

At a meeting in Hamilton on 12.12.1983 we were led back again to the book of Ezra. Ezra 1:5 'everyone whose heart God had moved'. As in Ezra's day, Cyrus's edict was for all displaced Jews to return, but as today, only a minority caught the specific vision that had gripped Ezra's heart. In the things of God numbers do not count, but only purity of heart.

Ezra 7:8; 10:9: because Ezra was so taken up with legitimate religious business, it took four and a half months to discover the sin of the people. The devil would have God's people so busy with legitimate traditions that we miss God's priority.

> Satan dreads nothing but prayer. His one desire is to keep saints from praying. He fears nothing from prayerless studies, prayerless work, prayerless religion. He laughs at our toil, mocks at our wisdom, but he trembles when we pray (Samuel Chadwick).

> God is about to send revival to His people. Our task is to provide the prayer ramp over which his purposes can pass (Selwyn Hughes).

Looking back, I wonder at the wisdom God gave a 'wee housewife from Hamilton'.

The promise from Ezra 6:8 was practised for a number of years and God was faithful. Then my faith wavered and I gave in to worry and anxiety and did what I had said I would never do. As a committee we did our own thing and disobeyed the Lord. Looking back I believe God was testing our faith. It's so easy to have faith and trust in God when things are going well, but what happens when 'though the fig tree should not blossom, nor the fruit be on the vines, the produce of the olive fail and the fields yield no food, the flock be cut off from the fold and there be no herd in the stalls, yet I will rejoice in the Lord; I will take joy in the God of my salvation' (Hab. 3:17-18, ESV).

Michael Baughan in his book *The Prayer Principle* puts it into a modern city equivalent: 'Though my business schemes fail, profits become losses, I lose my job, my bank balance dwindles to nothing, and I cannot see where I am going to get another job or how I'm going to be able to support my family, yet I will rejoice in the Lord!' How is your faith in these circumstances?

My husband, Peter, was a self-employed business-man. Throughout our business life, we often struggled financially, especially in the early days when accounts would not be paid for three months. With no other in-come, things were often tough. **BUT GOD** never failed us. I have marked in my Bible against these verses in Habakkuk several dates, with remarks such as, no mon-ey, car not selling, no work, but also against 'I will re-joice' in large letters is YES LORD! God gave us the faith to trust and believe that even when the skies are not blue and the tunnel is long and dark, he is still God and to know him and trust him pleases him (Heb. 11:6).

And yet here at another stage in my Christian life, my faith wavered. The issue was money. Prayer Chain costs money and as its ministry increased so did its expenses. From its inception any donations were tithed according to Scripture's principle, but as time went on and our bills grew larger, that ceased to be our practice. No decision was taken. Tithing just lapsed. Financially things became dire and eventually the decision was taken to ask members to make an annual subscription. In my heart I knew this was wrong and a deep and lasting sadness overwhelmed me. But even the subscription income did not pay the bills.

The Minutes make depressing reading. 'A shortfall in expected income from annual subscriptions has led to a situation where Prayer Chain was unable to meet all its financial commitments.'

Temporary loans enabled the payment of outstanding bills. It was also agreed to suspend production of the Bulletin. How true it is that when we obey the Lord we get results, when we disobey him we get consequences! At the same time we were seeking charitable status, which would have made such a difference to our situation. But for two years, each time it was discussed by the government department it was referred back to us for one reason or another. We struggled on. Now again, in our time of need, I reread the book of Ezra and immediately saw parallels with our situation. God seemed to show me that it was not my problem to worry about the money we needed. If it was his work he would supply the funding. This was reinforced at a conference in Birmingham where I was challenged to be obedient to the Lord.

I went home and called a meeting of the Committee. The Minutes record what happened. There was 'a wide-ranging discussion on the whole question of funding Prayer Chain. Some members were very resistant to any imposed giving; others were willing and anxious to pay more, especially to reinstate the Bulletin. Any appeals to give to the work should be on the grounds of a love offering, not a legal contraction.'

When pressure came from different quarters to ask for a subscription I gave in, and we as a committee 'did not enquire of the LORD' (Josh. 9:14). We were disobedient. That chapter of the book of Joshua tells what happened when Joshua did not enquire of the Lord. God had promised to give the children of Israel the whole land of Canaan, having commanded Moses first to wipe out all its inhabitants. When the Gibeonites heard this they planned to deceive Joshua, Moses' successor. To make it look as though they had travelled a great distance, and were therefore not inhabitants of Canaan, they loaded their donkeys with worn-out old sacks and cracked and mended wineskins. Wearing patched clothes and ancient sandals they carried moulded food, dry as a bone. The men of Israel, including Joshua, were taken in by their deception. And they did not enquire of the Lord. 'Joshua made a treaty of peace with them to let them live' (Josh. 9:15).

Contrast that with the story of Jehoshaphat in 2 Chronicles 20. When he heard that the Moabites and Ammonites were coming to make war, anxious though he was, he resolved to 'enquire of the LORD' (2 Chron. 20:3). Jehoshaphat stood before all the assembly and sought the Lord, reminding them that they had no power to face what was ahead of them except the power of the Lord. God wonderfully answered them, reminding them that the battle was not theirs but his. And he gave them victory. As the old hymn says,

> O what peace we often forfeit,
> O what needless pain we bear,
> All because we do not carry
> Everything to God in prayer.
> (Joseph Scriven)

We knew we had been disobedient to God's promise from Ezra that we were to rely on him and the funds for his work would be met from his royal treasury. After that long discussion at committee regarding our finances, 1 Chronicles 29 was read. It records the gifts that were given for the building of the temple. And the chapter became a pivotal one in the life of Prayer Chain.

> King David said... 'The task is great, because this palatial structure is not for man but for the Lord God. With all my resources I have provided for the temple of my God ...' Then the leaders of families, the officers of the tribes of Israel, the commanders of thousands and commanders of hundreds, and the officials in charge of the king's work gave willingly... David praised the Lord in the presence of the whole assembly, saying 'Praise be to you, O Lord, God of our father Israel, from everlasting to everlasting. Yours, O Lord, is the greatness and the power and the glory and the majesty and the splendour, for everything in heaven and earth is yours. Yours, O Lord, is the kingdom, you are exalted as head over all.... O Lord our God, as for all this abundance that we have provided for building you a temple for your Holy Name, it comes from your hand, and all of it belongs to you ... All these things have I given willingly and with honest intent. And now I have seen with joy how willingly your people who are here have given to you.'

We were broken. A time of corporate repentance followed and it was agreed that the annual subscription should be withdrawn. A short while later, a decision to implement the practice of tithing was taken. One-tenth of all income would be given away, the cause, or individual recipient, to be decided at each committee meeting. That very day, just after we had repented, the mail arrived at the office and there among it was a letter informing us we had received charitable status. We wept tears of gratitude and praised God for his goodness and for confirming the rightness of our decision in such a timely way. I can still feel the thrill I felt that day. Praise the Lord! A day or two later we received a £300 donation and from that day to this the Lord has met our needs.

A much-happier Minute records a meeting some time later. 'Income increased from £4,285 in the previous year to £7,222, and expenditure dropped from £3,046 to £1,771. There was a balance of £6,060. Substantial gifts have come in since the committee repented of asking for money via subscriptions.' We had learned a hard lesson and we were fighting on the right side once again.

> Trust and obey
> For there's no other way
> To be happy in Jesus
> But to trust and obey.
>
> But we never can prove
> The delights of his love
> Until all on the altar we lay.
> For the favour he shows
> And the love he bestows
> Are for them who will trust and obey.
>
> (John Henry Sammis)

On what, someone might ask, did a telephone prayer chain ministry run up bills anyway? Having organised everything from my kitchen table for seven years, there came a point when enough was enough. Papers, letters and files spilled everywhere and it took a marathon tidy to prepare the kitchen to be used as a kitchen! But as our need arose, God rose to meet it. A friend had a suite of offices in Royal Exchange Place in Glasgow, the upper floor of which he gave over to Christian ministries. In answer to our prayers he was moved to give us a tiny office there.

Another friend, whose business was office equipment, donated a computer, filing cabinets, a telephone answering machine, even pens and staples. My kitchen table nearly floated in the air having been relieved of its weight of papers! But it is still my Bethel, the place where I meet with my Master every day. Such gifts were showered on us that we were able to move in at no cost to the ministry, but offices cost money to run. The Lord, from his Royal treasury, has met postage, printing, phone, heating, lighting: all these and more.

Over the following two years we outgrew our tiny office – but just across the landing from us was a larger one, which was empty. I kept looking in the door and thinking how wonderful it would be if we could move in there. Having brought the matter to the Committee, I phoned the owner who said we could move right in. That was Monday. On Tuesday a friend gave us carpeting and laid it with Peter's help. By Wednesday we were in, up and running. Since then we have had a further move, to the Christian Resource Centre where we share a floor with Care. It is good to have that contact with other believers. Along with the several other ministries in the building, we enjoy a monthly prayer lunch when we have a time of sharing and prayer for each other's work and personal needs.

The ladies involved in Prayer Chain in Scotland come from all over the country. It therefore seemed important to meet together nationally as well as locally. So began our annual conferences and these too involved expense as venues had to be booked and speakers' costs refunded. Some of our speakers came from far afield. Evelyn Christenson even crossed the Atlantic several times to teach us further on the subject of prayer.

Since 1981 I have had the wonderful privilege of working with women from different backgrounds and denominations. Some, like Dr Winifred Anderson, have served the Lord for many years. She spent four decades working for him in Nepal. When she could have retired she chose instead to have a 'retread' and became our regional leader in Glasgow until she, with great reluctance and aged ninety, passed it on to someone else. We benefitted so much from her wisdom.

One of the blessings of Prayer Chain has been the unity and love we share. Each week our office is staffed by volunteers, some of whom travel a distance and others are from the Glasgow area. Coming with hearts prepared to know God's burden for our nation, we first spend time together in our little kitchen, asking him to confirm to us what he wants us to pray. Only after that do we fax and phone regional leaders and activate Prayer Chain.

Our conferences are not just large group teaching sessions, they are also where individual problems are met and dealt with. At our very first conference a group leader broke down and wept. 'What's wrong?'

I enquired a little anxiously. 'I just can't pray for people I don't know,' she explained through her tears, 'I don't know what's behind the situations we are praying about.' Scripture tells us that when we rely on the Lord he gives us the words we should speak. He did. 'It is like dropping a pebble in a pool,' I heard myself say, even though I'd not thought of the likeness before. 'The calls go out to lots of women,' I said, 'and if each asks the Lord to give a burden for the person they are praying for, so many things in that person's life will be covered by prayer just like the ripples spreading out on a pool.' She seemed to grasp what I was saying when I concluded that God alone knows what is happening in the background of anyone's life, and knows his will for each one.

Just a day or two after that conversation a letter arrived from another leader saying that she was too busy to remain on Prayer Chain. Sensing that there was more to it than that, I phoned, and a little encouragement enabled her to tell me that she too was having difficulties praying for people she did not know. I shared my thoughts with her, then told her I'd do nothing with her letter for a month when we would talk again. The following day she phoned to tell me to tear up her letter. A call had come through the previous evening to pray for a man who had cancer and for his family too. 'I just asked God to give me a burden for his family,' she explained. 'And do you know?' she went on excitedly, 'I touched the gate of heaven last night.' She stayed on.

Printing was another item of expense but a necessary one. From its early days Prayer Chain produced a Bulletin. But it was not born painlessly. I remember sitting in my garden struggling, really struggling, to put one of the early Bulletins together. A friend who called got the brunt of it. 'I can't do this,' I grumbled, 'I left school at fifteen. I can't write.' 'What's that you are holding in your hand?' she asked. I looked down. 'A pen,' I replied, puzzled. 'And what's in it?' she went on. 'Ink.' 'Think about it, Jessie,' my wise friend counselled. 'It is the ink that does the writing not the pen. You are just that pen and without the ink you are nothing. The Holy Spirit is the ink. He'll do the work, not you.' I would love to say that I found preparing the Bulletin easy ever afterwards. I didn't. But what she said stuck in my mind and encouraged me to seek the Lord's guidance and help in the job.

The Bulletin has changed a lot over the years, not least because of technology. Long gone are the days of typewriter and duplicator. Desktop publishing has taken over and made a vast difference to its appearance. But substantially it is much the same, although in its early years there was more stress on praying for individuals rather than for issues. Now most individuals are prayed for through their home region rather than nationally.

Bulletins are made up of items for prayer, answers to prayer and some teaching about prayer. Comparing two, fifteen years apart, is an interesting exercise. In 1982 we were encouraged by the following account. 'One of our Prayer Chain members was so moved by the testimony of X, a young Muslim convert to Christianity, that she requested prayer on his behalf, then wrote to tell him we were praying for him. Trained as a Mullah (Muslim priest) before his conversion, X is now doing Christian work in a predominantly Muslim area. He has known persecution and has even been beaten badly for his faith.

> On the day he received the letter telling him we were praying for him, he was so discouraged that he was on the verge of giving up his new faith. But the knowledge that hundreds of women were praying for him restored his courage and with renewed faith he turned again to God.'

The year 1997 saw another encouraging item in the Bulletin, now called Chain-link. 'My name is Vladimir, I am forty years old. I have a son, Alex, who is thirteen years old. His Mom, my wife, died three years ago. I cannot describe what it was like to lose my wife when she was thirty-five years old. But after my wife was taken from me I asked God why she suffered so much and why I watched her suffer for two years. Natasha was a kidney patient on dialysis. God answered in my spirit that it was my wife's privilege to share in the suffering of Christ. More than that, it was my great privilege to watch her sufferings. It reminded me of Jesus' suffering on the cross, and also of the Father's suffering watching his Son dying. It also brought a great comfort into my life that Natasha is with the Lord.

At the time of her home call, God gave me verses from 2 Corinthians 1:3-6. 'Praise be to the God and Father of our Lord Jesus Christ, the Father of compassion and the God of ALL comfort, who comforts us in all our troubles, so that we can comfort those in any trouble with the comfort we ourselves have received from God. For just as the sufferings of Christ flow over into our lives, so also through Christ our comfort overflows. If we are distressed, it is for your comfort and salvation; if we are comforted, it is for your comfort, which produces in you patient endurance of the same sufferings we suffered.' I want to comfort especially those who have lost their beloved ones with the comfort I've received. And also to challenge each of you not to be ashamed to comfort others with the comfort you have already...NOW! Please pray for me and my son.

The 1982 Bulletin exhorted prayer for the medical profession, outlining different areas of need and laying them before the Great Physician.

Fifteen years later the focus was on children and thirteen ways to pray for them. It is worth recording.

1. Pray they will receive Christ early in life – 2 Timothy 3:15.

2. Pray they will have a hatred of sin – Psalm 51:10.

3. Pray they will be caught when guilty – Psalm 119:71.

4. Pray they will be protected from the evil one – John 17:15.

5. Pray they will have a responsible attitude – Daniel 6:3.

6. Pray they will desire the right kind of friends, and be protected from wrong friends – Proverbs 1:10 & 15.

7. Pray they will be kept from the wrong mate and saved for the right one – 1 Corinthians 6:15-17.

8. Pray they will be kept pure as well as the one they will marry – 1 Corinthians 6:18-20.

9. Pray they will totally submit to God and turn from Satan – James 4:7.

10. Pray they will be willing to be sold out for Jesus – Romans 12:1-2.

11. Pray they will have a heart to obey the Lord – 1 Chronicles 29:19.

12. Pray that the Holy Spirit will be poured out on them – Isaiah 44:3-5.

13. Pray that they will be recognised as children whom the Lord has blessed – Isaiah 61:9.

With such practical prayers we cannot be accused of being so heavenly minded that we are of no earthly use.

The Bulletin, our conferences, the office, all these and much more became integral parts of our ministry. And they all cost money. But God who gave the vision in the beginning provided the resources throughout. Only when we took our eyes off him did our income fall short of our expenses. That was a salutary lesson but such a valuable one.

9

'I will be with you,' God said.
And he was.

When sorrows come,
They come not single spies,
But in battalions.
(William Shakespeare)

From time to time ill health has set me aside, but these times have been used by God to speak to me. When Karen was a toddler, I had viral meningitis and after two weeks of treatment developed an allergy to the drug I was taking. So unwell was I that one day I fainted, landing badly and fracturing my nose and a bone in my spine, cracking two ribs and covering myself with bruises. Only after ten days in hospital was I fit for nasal surgery and over the twelve months that followed I had four more operations. I sought the Lord, instead of asking him 'why?' I asked him 'what?'

God 'will sit as a refiner and purifier of silver; he will purify the Levites and refine them like gold and silver. Then the LORD will have men who will bring offerings in righteousness' (Mal. 3:3) spoke powerfully to me.

A poem by Ella Wheeler Wilcox expresses true qualities at times when it is hard to smile.

It is easy enough to be pleasant when life flows by like a song

But the woman (or man) worthwhile is the one who
can smile
When everything goes dead wrong.

I began to learn that God often uses suffering to bring
us to the point of obedience. Even Jesus, the sinless Son
of God, walked along that road, 'Although he was a son,
he learned obedience from what he suffered' (Heb. 5:8).
God's purpose in taking us through the valley of
suffering is to refine us and make us more like Jesus.

How thankful I am that God himself is our Refiner-
Purifier. He tempers the heat and is in control of the
furnace, knowing the exact temperature needed to
make the gold and silver in our lives pure so that our
faith 'of greater worth than gold, which perishes even
though refined by fire – may be proved genuine and
may result in praise, glory and honour when Jesus
Christ is revealed' (1 Pet. 1:7).

Someone gave me this poem. I don't know who
wrote it, but I say 'Amen' to its sentiment.

He sat by a furnace of sevenfold heat
As he watched by the precious ore,
And closer he bent with a searching gaze
As he heated it more and more.

He knew he had ore that could stand the test
And he wanted the finest gold,
To mould as a crown, for the King to wear,
Set with gems of price untold.

So he laid our gold in the burning fire
Tho' we fain would say him 'nay';
And he watched the dross that we had not seen
As it melted and passed away.

And the gold grew brighter and yet more bright,
But our eyes were dim with tears.
We saw the fire not the Master's hand,
And questioned with anxious fears.

Yet our gold shone out with a richer glow
As it mirrored a Form above,
That bent o'er the fire, tho' unseen by us
With a look of ineffable love.

Can we think it pleases his loving heart
To cause us a moment's pain?
Ah, no, but he sees through the present cross
The bliss of eternal gain.

So he waited there with a watchful eye,
With a love that is strong and sure;
And his gold did not suffer a bit more heat
Than was needed to make it pure.
(From **Streams in the Desert** devotional)

In November 1985 God gave me a hunger to know him in a deeper way. Two Scriptures spoke particularly powerfully to me. 'I want to know Christ and the power of his resurrection and the fellowship of sharing in his sufferings, becoming like him in his death, and so, somehow, to attain to the resurrection from the dead' (Phil. 3:10-11). And 'With flattery he will corrupt those who have violated the covenant, but the people who know their God will firmly resist him' (Dan. 11:32). I prayed that the Lord would become more real to me and that I would grow in my knowledge and love of him. Had I known how God would answer that prayer I might have thought twice about praying it!

Two months later, at the beginning of the following year, I prayed a prayer and recorded it in my diary.

'Father, let this year be one of the greatest I have ever known, especially in terms of my spiritual growth. Please help me, Lord, to be bold and strong for you, not to be afraid to stand up and be counted. Give me patience to cope with everything the enemy would do to me, or within my family, to dishearten and discourage. For every plan you have for me, give me holy wisdom not to thwart your divine will and purpose, but help me to walk so close to you that your voice will be heard and obeyed under all circumstances.' Little did I know how God was going to answer that prayer in the year that lay ahead.

The family all succumbed to flu. They recovered. I did not. The virus badly affected my heart, necessitating six weeks of bed rest. Had I thought about it in advance, I could have seen the frustrations I might have felt lying upstairs in bed while Peter, and Kirsteen and Graham who were grown up but still at home, coped downstairs. What a lot I would have found to worry about as I listened to their comings and goings. Were they remembering this? Had they done that? How different the truth was. They were welcome to get on with it as I basked in the love of the Lord. As soon as I was fit enough I read, prayed, meditated and enjoyed the Lord. I even caught up with my letter writing! God used that time of being set aside to answer my prayer to come to know him in a deeper way.

At the end of May, Shona came with her husband Kenny and their two children, Gavin and Katie, to spend a few days with us. As they left I remember turning to Peter and saying, 'This is the first time I've felt really well this year'. 'Let's go for a picnic tomorrow then,' he suggested. The following morning I had just one thing to do before we left, that was to book Glasgow City Halls for an evening of 'Prayer for the Nation'. Brian Mills and his team had agreed to come and lead the event. That done, we were free to go. Taking the car to Rosebank in Clydeside I thrilled at the beauty of God's creation. The spring flowers were in bloom and the fruit trees hung heavy with blossom. It was almost worth the weeks indoors to get the full impact of the glories of spring. Peter parked the car and we walked into the May sunshine. A few steps of beauty and pure enjoyment ... then I went over on my ankle. Peter heard the crack as clearly as I did. Neither of us needed to see the X-ray to know it was broken.

How fickle is the human heart. From enjoying a time apart and with the Lord I plummeted into the depths of depression. 'What is God playing at?' I demanded. Had I not just that morning booked a big venue for an evening of prayer? What more did he want? Did God not understand that this was a huge leap of faith for Prayer Chain? I could not read my Bible, neither could I pray. And the only Scripture verse I could remember was, 'He has walled me in so that I cannot escape' (Lam. 3:7).

Over the years I have tried to hide my times of depression from Peter and the family. But that probably only made it more difficult for them, as they were unable to draw near to me in my need when I could not admit the depths of my need to them. I withdrew from them and they had no way of getting close to me. Yet all I longed for was someone who would sit with me where I was, someone who would listen and would not accuse.

Joyce Hugget, in her book *Listening to Others*, gives expression to my thoughts.

'A depressed person needs someone who will not tire of listening to their main topic of conversation: themselves. Someone who will assure them that, even though they, the listener, may have nothing useful to say, they are prepared to stay in the darkness with the person suffering from depression until they emerge eventually from the tunnel's end.'

David Augsburger in *Caring Enough to Hear and be Heard* describes this patient listening well: 'When hearing is done as an act of caring, it is a healing process. The exact nature of this process will remain forever a mystery, a gift of grace for which we become profoundly grateful as we see it occurring, before which we are rightly humble as we know we have, in small measure, participated in it ... In caring-hearing, the hurt is opened, the festering bitterness of resentful illusions, the burning of angry demands, the numb frozenness of grief, the staleness of depression are allowed to drain. The light is allowed to pour in; sterilizing the infections and stimulating cells of hope and trust to begin new growth.'

In my confused mental state I fell prey to Satan's lies, thinking that a Christian, and the leader of Prayer Chain no less, should not get depressed, as though somehow believers were superhuman. While I struggled unsuccessfully to be aware of the presence of God, if the truth be told, there were times when I could have thrown the towel in. Have you ever felt like doing just that?

Looking back now on this time I realize that nothing comes into our lives by accident and no matter how bad it makes us feel it doesn't come to stay. I love these four little words found in the Bible – *it came to pass!* Someone has said if you don't feel the Presence of the Lord, who has moved? Certainly not the Lord.

Although I could not feel him there, my loving Father was beside me through it all and in time he gave me strength to read my Bible again. The first words I read hit me like a bolt of lightning. 'You broaden the path beneath me, so that my ankles do not turn over' (Ps. 18:36). What! 'If you didn't do this to me,' I asked the Lord, 'then who did?' He gave me another verse of Scripture. '[H]e will command his angels concerning you to guard you in all your ways; they will lift you up in their hands, so that you will not strike your foot against a stone' (Ps. 91:11-12). The truth hit me. It was Satan himself who was attacking. 'Why?' I asked myself, but not for long, the answer was clear. It had been God's will that the meeting in Glasgow City Halls should go ahead. And such was the devil's concern about the prayer that would result from it that he determined to wreck the event, starting with wrecking me. I would love to say that I snapped out of the depression right away. It was not like that. But I did begin to get better as I focused on the Lord.

> I had a battle fierce today
> Within my place of prayer,
> I went to meet and talk with God
> But I found Satan there.

He whispered, 'You can't really pray
You lost out long ago,
You might say words while on your knees
But you can't pray you know.'

So then I pulled my helmet down,
Way down upon my ears,
And found it helped to still his voice
And helped allay my fears.

I checked my other armour o'er,
My feet in peace were shod,
My loins with truth were girded round,
My sword, the word of God.

My righteous breastplate still was on
My heart's love to protect,
My shield of faith was all intact,
His fiery darts bounced back.

I called on God in Jesus' name,
I pled the precious blood,
While Satan sneaked away in shame
I met and talked with God.
(Anon)

That experience taught me a valuable lesson. The devil is a strategist. God's Word says, 'One day the angels came to present themselves before the LORD, and Satan also came with them. The LORD said to Satan, "Where have you come from?" Satan answered the Lord, "From roaming through the earth and going to and fro in it."' (Job 1:6-7). We might be sure that Satan was not wandering aimlessly, rather he was searching for evidences of God's work that he might attack and try to destroy. And he is no different today.

I am often surprised by the fact that many believers do not fully understand that we are in a spiritual conflict. We have been brought from the kingdom of darkness into the kingdom of light and these two kingdoms, the kingdom of God and the kingdom of Satan, are in direct opposition to each other.

The unseen enemy of prayer is real. Satan himself is the prince of the power of the air. '… where in times past you walked … according to the prince of the power of the air. The spirit that now works in the children of disobedience' (Eph. 2:2, AV). Satan is permitted within bounds to tempt, hinder and accuse the children of God. Peter encourages us to 'Be self-controlled and alert. Your enemy the devil prowls around like a roaring lion looking for someone to devour' (1 Pet. 5:8), and we read in 1 Thessalonians that Paul was hindered by Satan from seeing the Thessalonians.

Job was the target of Satan. He lived a blameless and upright life, but God permitted Satan to test him severely. Although Job suffered deeply, and lost everything material, his faith in God never wavered. He could say in the midst of tremendous testing, 'But he knows the way that I take; when he has tested me, I shall come forth as gold' (Job 23:10). Satan was defeated, because 'greater is he that is in us than he that is in the world'.

I love the words Job spoke after he recounted all his sorrows, everyone had deserted him, even his intimate friends detested him and those he loved had turned away from him. He even felt that God's hand had struck him. 'Oh, that my words were recorded, that they were written on a scroll, that they were inscribed with an iron tool on lead, or engraved in rock for ever! I know that my Redeemer lives, and that in the end he will stand upon the earth. And after my skin has been destroyed, yet in my flesh I will see God; I myself will see him with my own eyes – I, and not another. How my heart yearns within me!' (Job 19:23-27). I'm sure that Job will be overwhelmed by the multitude of men and women in glory who will thank him for these wonderful words that have been such a blessing.

Satan's major goal is to be worshipped, to set himself above God. He is anti-church, but most of all anti-evangelism, anti-mission and especially anti-prayer. He will keep us so busy in legitimate activities, even Christian activities, that we have no time to pray down the power of God on our work. Or he will make us apathetic, enjoying our 'country club', asleep to the fact that men and women, boys and girls, are dying in their sins, and hell is filling. Spurgeon said, 'The devil is wide awake, why should we be asleep?'

Satan's strategy is deceit about the existence of warfare. We don't actually expect life to be lived out under battle conditions day in and day out. Many don't want to know that they are in a spiritual conflict. We are often unaware of it until long after the battle has been engaged and much ground has been won by the enemy. If we don't resist Satan he won't leave us and flee. These are the order of events. '**Submit** yourselves, then to God. **Resist** the devil, and he will flee from you. **Come near** to God and he will come near to you' (James 4:7, emphasis added).

Satan is very subtle; frontal attack is not his style. Preferring poison to gelignite, he has great success if he makes us feel down and out of sorts, burdened with life and joyless. He delights to hear us criticize one another, especially in our church. When there is controversy or factions within the church, he sits in a corner and laughs his head off. We are doing his work very well, thank you.

BUT GOD never sends us half-armed into battle, it is we who send ourselves out ill-equipped. God has given us all we need to stand against the enemy. Ephesians 6 (KJV) gives us our armour for battle. David Watson's book *God's Freedom Fighters* has been a great blessing in explaining our armour.

Putting on the first three pieces is basic preparation for battle. '... Stand therefore, **HAVING** your loins girt about with truth, [v. 14] and **HAVING** put on the breastplate of righteousness; And your feet shod with the preparation of the gospel of peace [v. 15] ... **TAKE** the helmet of salvation, and the sword of the Spirit [v. 17]' (emphasis added). David Watson explains it beautifully. 'A soldier is sitting in his tent waiting for the battle call. He has on his belt, his breastplate, and his boots. Suddenly the bugle calls. He picks up his shield; he puts on his helmet and he grasps his sword. He is ready for battle.'

The belt is the girdle of truth. We should deal with everything untruthful that would hinder us in the fight: any shade of dishonesty, deceit, exaggeration, pretence or half-truth. Jesus said that the truth would make us free. He is TRUTH; we must get to know him. The breastplate of righteousness is Christ. We must trust him for the grace to think and act rightly in our relationships with each other. We should have holiness of life and character.

Our gospel sandals enable us to hold our ground in the defence of the gospel. *Feet, readiness* and *gospel* all speak of carrying the 'Good News' to others, whether people in faraway places or our next-door neighbours. In Matthew 28 we are given our commission, in Ephesians 6 we are given our equipment for battle. We must be prepared for battle. Our wills must be brought into play, so that when the enemy attacks we are not caught unaware. Our hearts and minds are ready when he comes at us subtly, and faith comes readily into action as we take up the shield of faith. Our thoughts are brought into captivity as we put on our helmet and grasp our sword, which is the Word of God, and wield it to inflict blows on the enemy. The Word of God is the only defensive weapon listed in Paul's arsenal of spiritual weaponry. All others are offensive.

Satan would also deceive us as to our location in battle. If we think of ourselves as the battleground, we will see ourselves as the battle spoils. Christians fight on three battlefields: the **world,** the **flesh** and the **devil.** We are bombarded by the world daily, through the battlefields of the media and our circumstances.

Then there is the flesh – our carnal thinking, material desires, personal pride and giving in to temptation. I find that my mind is a major battlefield daily. A word can be said that triggers thoughts in my mind, and I can have a skirmish as thoughts become completely outrageous. From time to time someone just needs to say something to me and then there is a major battle and the devil wins a victory.

We often blame the devil when it is the flesh that is the problem. But as we have said, he plays a major role in deceiving us, in harassing us and in hindering us. **BUT GOD** has given us the victory over Satan. Our location in this battle is **from victory.** We do not fight **for victory.** The victory was won at Calvary when Jesus defeated Satan. We need not fear if we have on the whole armour of God, we can stand firm, for God is with us.

Elisha's servant was very afraid by the sight of the great army that surrounded the city. Elisha prayed and the Lord opened the servant's eyes to see 'the hills full of horses and chariots of fire all round Elisha' (2 Kings 6:17). When Joshua was preparing to do battle with Jericho a man appeared before him with a drawn sword. Joshua learned that 'he was the Commander of the army of the Lord'. He was none other than the Lord himself. The Prince of Peace assured Joshua of victory over the enemy. I do not fully understand why or how our participation in prayer turns the tide of battle, but there are many instances in Scripture that give credence to this fact, and there are people today who can firmly prove that prayer has been used to change their circumstances.

I wonder if it is significant that we read of much satanic activity during the Lord's life on earth. The Gospels record many evidences of demon possession. Could it be that, because the Lord of creation spent those thirty-three years as a human being, holding out his free offer of salvation to those whom he met, Satan and all his angels were frenetic in their efforts to thwart the Lord's work? In Christ the victory over Satan was won. And the battle we fight today is fought from a position of victory rather than one where the outcome is uncertain. But sometimes when a soldier is in the thick of a battle he loses sight of the overall war.

So it was with me. Satan engaged in a battle for my mind and I became so caught up in it that I took my eyes off the Captain of my Salvation and the fact that he has won the war, and the conflict is all but over. Perhaps it is because I'm a housewife that I tend to see things in homely pictures. Or it might be that I've catered for so many people over the years that my mind has just turned a little! But a picture of a sandwich came to me. And I saw the two slices of bread being pressed hard together, so hard that the filling squirted out from between them and the two pieces of bread lay together. It made me think of my relationship with the Lord. When he draws near to me and I to him there is no room for Satan in-between. 'Resist the devil, and he will flee from you. *Draw near to God* and He will draw near to you' (James 4:7-8, NASB, emphasis added).

Evenings of Prayer for the Nation did take place in October that year. Eight hundred and fifty men and women gathered to pour out their concerns to the Lord. A further 300 met in Edinburgh and 260 in Dundee. No wonder Satan was anxious. With over 1400 people praying he had good reason to be.

The family gathered just before Christmas and, while playing with my grandchildren, I fell and hurt my hand. Thinking nothing of it I got on with the celebrations. It was my son-in-law who questioned me about my wrist; being a doctor he noticed I was in pain, and insisted on it being X-rayed. His suspicions were correct; it was broken. Satan overstepped himself that time. Focusing on the Lord I asked him how he was going to use this new challenge. And as 1987 dawned I looked forward to finding out. What plans my Father had for me!

An invitation came to speak at the Parliamentary Wives Christian Fellowship. Aged fifty-four, and feeling totally inadequate for the task God had called me to do, I was reassured by words I had read in Catherine Marshall's book, *Beyond Ourselves*: 'Crisis brings us face to face with our inadequacy and our inadequacy in turn leads us to the inexhaustible sufficiency of God. This is the power of helplessness, a principle written into the fabric of life.'[1] Little did I know how God was going to use my helplessness in the days ahead to show his almighty power made perfect in total weakness.

I travelled south in the worst snowstorm for years. Had I booked to fly, which had been suggested, I should not have got there as the road to the airport was closed. Because it was less expensive, I intended to go by train and just made it to the station before the roads were blocked by snow. I arrived in London two hours late and four changes later. It was not the easiest of journeys; suitcases and a fractured wrist still in plaster are not the best of friends.

The meeting was held in a room directly under Big Ben, in one of the apartments of the Speaker of the House of Commons. Beautifully refurbished, it took my breath away. There was a bed in it, one Queen Victoria slept in. Should the Queen and Prince Philip ever need to stay in the Palace of Westminster, it is the one they would sleep in too.

Somehow it seemed out of place, but none the less comfortable, to sit with the Parliamentary wives around the splendid table in that room, packed lunches, mugs of tea an' all! There were about fifteen ladies present, and I shared with them my testimony of how Prayer Chain was born of God and how the idea might relate to them.

When the meeting was over I went back to one of their homes where we had a time of prayer. As we prayed I developed a headache, the like of which I had never had before. 'I think you should call a doctor,' I heard myself say to Susie when she finished praying. And with that I lapsed into a coma, which was to last ten days. I had suffered a cerebral haemorrhage. When Kenny, my son-in-law, discussed it with Peter that evening it was in terms of there being three likely outcomes: I could be left paralysed, require brain surgery or I might die.

Peter, on hearing the news, poured out his heart in prayer. And God spoke to him through two verses of the Bible. 'Wake up! Strengthen what remains, and is about to die, for I have not found your deeds complete in the sight of God' (Rev. 3:2), and 'This sickness will not end in death. No, it is for God's glory' (John 11:4, KJV). A friend was also given these verses and shared them with Peter to his great comfort. He took the Lord at his word. Peter got someone to help dig his car out of the snow before taking him to the airport for a flight to London. Arriving in the capital he went to Miles and Patricia's flat on his way to the hospital. **But God** knew the plans he had for us.

Our friends were not at home but their Peruvian maid was. Peter must surely have felt overwhelmed when she confided in him, 'I can give you two Scriptures the Lord has given me for Mrs McFarlane. He has given me John 11:4, 'This sickness is not unto death, but for the glory of the Lord.' And he has given me Revelation 3:2, 'Wake up! Strengthen what remains and is about to die, for I have not found your deeds complete in the sight of my God.' God had spoken.

God had not only spoken, he had acted too. **But God** knew the plans he had for us.

Looking back I can see his preparations as far back as 1984 when we met Miles and Patricia at the London Prayer Breakfast. It was with them I stayed on the night before I spoke in Westminster. When I got my brain haemorrhage it was they who accompanied me to hospital. And their flat was to be Graham's home for the next seven weeks. He was studying for his PhD through King's College in London, but was working from home. What a blessing it was to have him free and able to visit me every day I was in hospital. God's wonderful provision, planned and purposed by his divine will years before, was being outworked. Why is it that we fear the future when it is in his sovereign hands?

Although in a coma, I was conscious of what was happening around me and heard what people were saying to me and about me. But most of all I was conscious of the presence of the Lord. Some time later I wrote down my memories of that experience. I cannot describe it any better now than I did then.

'The awesome presence of the living God was so real. I did not see flashing lights or a tunnel, or even the Lord, but I knew he was there. It seemed that I only needed to go through a door and I would have been with him. It was a beautiful experience, and I remember that I wanted to go, but thoughts of my family came to mind: my children, Shona and Kenny, Graham, Karen and Kirsteen, and my grandchildren, Gavin and Katie, and my husband Peter. I knew total submission to the will of God whatever that might be. Great peace.'

I heard two words, 'Go back'. Much of what happened during those first ten days is cloudy but what I have related remains crystal clear. Go back to where? Go back to what? These questions filled my mind many times. Was I about to die?

When I regained consciousness I had no vision, and was told I was to have complete bed rest, lying flat on my back for six to eight weeks, and that I would undergo brain surgery to seal off the leak in the artery that had caused the cerebral haemorrhage. My home for the next seven weeks was a little room, which I could not visualise because I was living in a world of black shadows. But my room was to become a haven of peace, not only for me but for my nurses and visitors too. One day, sensing someone had come into my room and sat on my bed I felt a depression on the mattress and called out. No-one answered. But I knew someone was there. I am sure it was the Lord. His presence was so real.

At this time three friends were led to battle for me in prayer. They felt assured that the Lord was going to heal me, that the healing would glorify God but that Satan would oppose his good purposes. They battled in prayer all day and on the following morning I awoke with my sight restored.

Peter visited me every weekend and how I looked forward to these times together. He brought me news of home and family – I missed them so much – also mail and 'goodies' from friends. Over the weeks in London I had visitors every day: friends from our church down on business, Parliamentary wives, as well as my sister Wilma. She and her husband, who were serving God with Operation Mobilisation in Zaventon, Belgium, were sent a gift specifically to enable her to fly over to visit me.

Nurses constantly came in and out of my room saying that there was something special about it they had never felt before. It was a joy to share with them that what they were sensing was the peace of God, and to tell them about Jesus. How God was glorified through all of this, and how many of these nurses were touched by him will only be revealed in eternity. I am sure that I did not do or say all that I could have done. There are always regrets. Looking back I wish I had given him more.

During this time I was still having severe headaches and feeling unwell. Lying flat on my back without a pillow, not being able to sit up for meals or go to the toilet, having my hair washed over the back of the bed: all these made life difficult, but they are not the things I remember most. I remember the elderly lady who came into my room every week to water my flowers and the little Filipino maid who cleaned my room, and who asked Peter where he and I had learned to speak such good English!

One day, when my headache was very bad, the wives of two Members of Parliament came to visit. They asked me how I was feeling and I told them about my headache. One of them, Sylvia Mary, put her hands above my head, not touching me, and began to pray.

She prayed first in English, then in a tongue, then in English. As she prayed I could feel a heat going into my head. Also as she prayed I saw a picture of a brain with its arteries and with a flood lying at the base of the skull. As Sylvia Mary prayed, I saw the flood disappear into the arteries. When she had finished praying, my friend asked, 'Did you feel that heat?' I said I had. But I did not tell her about the picture I had seen. Because the denomination to which I belong does not practise speaking in tongues or encourage visions I thought it was only my imagination. But it was real.

When I wakened each morning I felt a big black cloud resting on me, a cloud of fear of what the future held. Would I be paralysed? Would I be a vegetable after brain surgery? These questions flooded my thoughts. In my weakness I turned to the Lord, praying that he would do whatever he chose with my life.

Total surrender. Morning by morning I handed myself and my situation into the hands of my loving Father and focused my mind on the fact that although I did not know what my future held I knew God held my future. **But God** knew the plans he had for me and each morning I seemed to be given that picture of a brain in which a blood clot was disappearing. At the end of the week I had no choice but to say, 'Lord, I believe you have healed me.' Looking back, I am sorry I hadn't the courage to say it to the professor who was looking after me during my seven-week stay there.

I lay flat on my back knowing all the while I had been healed. Following a second angiogram the professor came to my bedside and said, 'We can find no trace of your haemorrhage, and no trace of where it came from.' It grieves me that I did not have the courage to tell him I knew that weeks ago. I missed that opportunity.

Having lain flat without even one pillow for seven weeks, it was a strange sensation when a nurse put the back of the bed up a bit and left me to sit for two hours. I was then wheeled into the 'well ward' and after a while a nurse helped me up. Before an hour had passed I was up and away, walking to the end of the ward by myself. 'Do you think I might get home tomorrow?' I asked the physiotherapist that afternoon. She took me to a flight of stairs which I walked up and down three times with no difficulty. The next day I was out of hospital. As I was leaving I had a further reminder of God's goodness: 'Do you know,' said my physiotherapist, 'only five per cent of patients leave here without having had brain surgery?' Peter drove down and two days later I was home. Home, sweet home!

How grateful Peter and I are for my bonus years and for the family blessings they have brought with them. Our eldest daughter, Shona, a schoolteacher, and her husband Kenny, who is a consultant surgeon, live in Kirkcaldy. Our grandson, Gavin, has just graduated with a PhD from St Andrews University. Gavin and Katie, his sister, our eldest granddaughter, and a joy to us, live in Edinburgh. My son, Graham, and his wife Hilary and granddaughter Flora live some distance from us in Gloucester. Graham is still lecturing at London Theological Seminary and Flora is a budding tennis player (look out Wimbledon in a few years!).

We are so fortunate to have Karen and our two granddaughters, Olivia and Niamh, living only minutes from us. Our youngest daughter, Kirsteen, lives with her partner Duncan near St Andrews. Because of distance and work we don't see them very often, but phone and email are busy each week! God spared me for a purpose. I have no choice but to live what is left of my life 100 per cent for him.

10

Passports please!

It is good to have an end to the journey,
but it is the journey that matters in the end.
(Anon)

When, in 1974, my friend told me she believed God had a speaking ministry for me, I found it hard to take her seriously. Time was to prove her right and me wrong. That was surprise enough, but God had more in store. I found myself travelling to places which were only names to me, as well as to some I'd never heard of. And it all started off at my kitchen table.

My concern for our nation moved me to pray, but it also moved me to act. Not knowing what to do, I decided to invite some people to my home on the 2nd April 1985 to discuss the situation as I saw it, people who were better informed than me and decidedly better connected. I shake my head when I think of my audacity. With Peter's agreement I sat at the kitchen table and wrote to five eminent churchmen explaining that I had something to share with them. I was not quite an unknown name to them because of the Luis Palau Mission and Prayer Chain. It transpired that these men had been meeting together for eight months in a group called Concern for Scotland, and that they were just about to invite me to join them. They asked me to share my burden at their next meeting. It was with fear and trembling that I did so, telling them that I was sure that prayer was the only way forward for Scotland, and that without it the church and the nation would not see God's blessing.

As a result of that meeting I became involved with Concern for Scotland which, in 1989, became the Evangelical Alliance (Scotland), and I had the privilege of serving on the Executive Committee for a few years with wonderful men and women of God. I was invited to be part of a Lausanne Group, meeting over two years in Edinburgh prior to the Lausanne Conference which was to be held in Manila in 1989. That needs some explanation, the names are so confusing that it seems as though places don't know where they are! After a congress organised by Billy Graham in Lausanne in 1974, it was decided to meet from time to time to consolidate the work done there. These meetings took place in different parts of the world and the 1989 one was scheduled to be held in Manila. The ripples from this congress were to be astounding. I was asked to hold a small seminar on prayer.

Not for a moment did I think I would be there, but I was. Prayer Chain's Minutes record, 'Jessie requests much prayer for her proposed visit to Manila. Among other things we should pray that the result of this conference should be for Scotland's spiritual good and revival. Twenty four delegates are going from Scotland.'

Four thousand people from 197 countries attended and I shared a workshop on prayer. We were there to pray together, to study and to discuss the way forward for world evangelism. I came home very excited about the manifesto which came out of Manila. It aimed to encourage Christians to reach the world for the Lord, starting with the people in their own communities. An American evangelist, Sammy Tippit, was at the conference. It was the first time we met but it was not to be the last. God was building networks of which we were not yet aware!

This conference had a tremendous impact on my life. It was such a blessing to mix with men and women from around the world, many who had suffered for the sake of Jesus. A visual reminder of this was right in the centre of the main conference hall where a section of thirty seats had been cordoned off. These seats should have been occupied by men and women from Russia who had been refused visas to enter the Philippines.

I will never forget the testimony of a Chinese pastor who had been imprisoned for his faith for many years. He constantly witnessed and could not be stopped. Pastor Chan was put to work in the cesspool but even there he would not be quiet. He sang all the time and, in a beautiful tenor voice, which rang out throughout the auditorium, he sang, 'I come to the garden alone, while the dew is still on the roses, and the voice I hear falling on my ear, the Son of God disposes. And he walks with me and he talks with me, and he tells me I am his own. And the joy we share as we tarry there, none other has ever known.' There was not a dry eye in the hall.

Another moving story was from a fourteen-year-old girl from Central China. She was one of nine young people who were arrested by communist cadres for preaching the gospel. They were beaten and forced to kneel all day and night. On the third day this girl fainted and the authorities released her. The others knelt in prison for eight nights and nine days. When she was reunited with them on their release she began to cry. They asked her why she was crying. 'You should be happy now that your friends are free.' She replied, 'They suffered for Jesus for nine days; I only suffered for three!'

Josef Monterengo, a Russian Pastor imprisoned for nine years, counted it a blessing being in bonds because three notorious gang leaders were converted through his witness and are now church leaders.

The powerful international chorus crying out at the conference was 'Get Ready, stop playing games, stop divisiveness, and turn complacency to enthusiasm. It has been nearly 2000 years since the Lord Jesus, by his Spirit established his church and said, "I will build my church and the gates of hell shall not prevail against it. Let us be a church working together to take the whole Gospel to the whole world."'

We came home inspired and fired up to do just that. Why has it not happened? Maybe we need to be in the shoes of those who have been through the fire of suffering and persecution to prevent us losing our apathy!

Three years later I was on my travels again, first to Brussels to a Prayer Leaders' Conference, then across the Atlantic for my first visit to the United States of America. I had been invited to be a delegate at a Prayer Leaders' World Conference to be held at Cove, Billy Graham's Conference Centre, high in the Blue Ridge

Mountains not far from the evangelist's home. Dr Graham, who had just returned from a mission in Russia, came with his wife, Ruth, to the conference for dinner. Never did I think I would meet these great warriors in the Lord's army.

After the conference I met up with Peter in Boston and we flew to San Antonio in Texas where I had an engagement to speak to women prayer leaders. God used that meeting to touch the lives of three women who went on to establish a women's prayer rally which meets twice yearly to pray for a day, for America. They too have a burden for their nation. God is gathering his armies in battle against Satan in many different parts of the world.

Time was when the thought of flying to Majorca was nearly enough to put me off going on holiday. I was afraid of flying. That was a problem God had to deal with if he was going to use me in different parts of the world. I committed it to him and he gave me victory over my fear. Some people think that the Bible is airy fairy. How wrong they are. It is the most practical of all books. In it I read that God said, 'For God hath not given us the spirit of fear; but of power, and of love' (2 Tim. 1:7, AV). I took God at his word, and knowing that he was with me relieved me of my fear of flying.

Conferences I attended in both Brussels and Vienna in 1993 were memorable, mainly because of the people I met. One of them, Elizabeth Middlestradt, edits a Christian magazine with a circulation of 10,000 in Germany, Romania and Hungary. God gave her a vision for Eastern Europe and I caught something of it. He laid it on my heart. And it was there too that

I met Mia Oglice. She and her husband translate God's Word and Christian books into Romanian, and Mia and I became prayer partners. How the Lord must have smiled as I clocked up air miles. Peter was very supportive and prayerful but it could not always have been easy for him, our lifestyle having changed so dramatically.

God did indeed take away my fear of flying. I flew alone from Glasgow to London then to California, from there up to Colorado Springs to an AD2000 Conference with fifteen women leaders from Kenya, Argentina, Malaysia, India, America, Australia and Africa. After that I went on to San Antonio and Atlanta, up to Chattanooga, back to Atlanta, on to Boston and then home via London. Wow! Who says God does not answer prayer!

While in Vienna I received an invitation to a Prayer Conference in California, a trip that was to make a huge impact on my life. The night before the conference I met with about twenty-five women, all of them beautifully dressed. I felt a real country bumpkin! We spent the evening praying together. The conference was held in the presidential suite of a grand hotel. And the President does actually stay there. I hope he appreciates the big television monitor in his bathroom!

For the next week I stayed with a wonderful lady who lived in Newport Beach, just down the road from John Wayne's widow. My friend Peggy was over seventy and had given her life to Jesus a few years before. As we spent time together I learned of the many hurts she had suffered, hurts that had been the means of bringing her to know the Saviour. Peggy's mother, sister and husband had all committed suicide. One of her daughters was living a life which brought much sadness to Peggy who, with tears in her eyes, related that her daughter had been in Las Vagas with an alcoholic boyfriend when her thirteen-year-old daughter died in Peggy's arms. She had also been estranged from her son for ten years.

As I listened to Peggy's story, I was amazed at how God's amazing powerful grace had kept her through all the trials, and was using her as a powerful witness, bringing glory to God. It was a week of very mixed blessings and I knew God was doing something in my life. It was an exercise of patience and resting in God. I felt much burdened to pray for Peggy's daughter, who was obviously very unhappy, and was delighted when she offered to run us to the Crystal Cathedral where I was invited to speak to the woman's Bible study. This was led by a lady who was at the conference in California, who has an MA in Theology from Fuller Seminary with a major in marriage and family, and is Minister of Caring for the Hour of Power International! I could only pray that God would water any seed sown and it would produce fruit for the kingdom of God.

Peggy took me to the John Wayne Airport in Orange County and I flew to Salt Lake City, where I waited for a plane to Colorado Springs; there I was met and taken to the Hideaway, where the AD2000 Leaders Conference was held. It was so good to meet up with Violet (Ivory Coast), Blossom (Jamaica), Juliet (India), Robin (Australia), Alina (Poland), and dear Evelyn Christenson and her friend Cathryn whom I had all met at a previous conference. Later I met Inonge from Zambia, Kai Yum from Malaysia, Ethel Hurr from the Netherlands and Kay Arthur. We prayed and planned together especially for Inonge, who might have become the next President of Zambia. After breakfast I was off again flying to Dallas, Fort Worth, to catch a plane to San Antonio.

I was met at the airport by Tex Tippitt and taken to meet the four other ladies who were organizing the meeting at Alamo City Baptist Church, and we spent the evening in prayer for the meeting next day. I knew that our prayers were answered as I stood up to speak as the presence of God was so real and God touched lives, twenty women came forward to dedicate their lives to Christ. After lunch I did a workshop on setting up a prayer chain.

Next day, we left at 8am for the Wayside Chapel where a day conference was to be held. Women from twenty-eight churches around San Antonio came, and again God blessed. Two ladies from Atlanta led the praise which was so full of worship and glorifying to the Lord. One was born with a cleft palate and could not speak or communicate until she had ten operations to rebuild her face. God has used her suffering to produce in her a wonderful ministry of song. I'm so glad God never wastes our sorrows! The other also has come though her 'Valley of Baca'. She was a drug abuser and sang in rock bands, but found release and peace in Jesus. She writes beautiful songs and their ministry was used to touch lives. As a result of God speaking especially to three women, he gave the vision of a yearly gathering of all the churches in San Antonio to pray for their city. This has continued through the years and is still growing.

The previous year, when Peter and I were on holiday, we went on a bus tour of Atlanta. One of the impressive buildings in the centre of the city had a neon sign round it advertising Coca Cola. There being little by way of historical monuments, the bus tour took us along Tuxedo Road to see the mansion houses there. Stopping outside one of them, it looked to me like the set for *Gone with the Wind*. Our driver told us that this had been the home of the man who invented Coca Cola. When, a year later, I was invited to speak at Coca Cola Mansions I thought it would be in the city centre building we had seen with its neon advertising. A surprise awaited me.

On arriving at the airport Jenny met me in the chauffeur-driven car and took me to her home. As we drove through the city, Jenny told me about herself and her husband, Guy, who was running for Governor, and a little about the house he had bought her. I could hardly believe my eyes when we turned off Tuxedo Road into the drive that led up to the house our bus driver had pointed out to us, the house which had previously belonged to the inventor of Coca Cola. But while it was a most beautiful mansion, like something out of a film, it was a home in which there was a sense of peace, and a lot of love.

Jenny has the heart of an evangelist and twice a week she holds a women's Bible class in the basement of her home and I had the privilege of speaking at one of its meetings. God is certainly no respecter of persons. In the meeting were ex-Governor's wives, women who worked in the Senate and key women in Atlanta. I share this with you, not to promote Jessie McFarlane, but to give glory to God, who can take an insignificant woman saved by his wonderful grace and allow her the privilege to be his servant! He can do the same for you!

Someone has said that the door of opportunity is marked 'Push', but I thank God that I have never needed to push any door. In Revelation 3:8 God speaks to the church in Philadelphia about opening doors that no one can shut. When God opens doors we have to recognize opportunities and then step out in faith, asking him for wisdom and the courage to act on them.

God has taken me to places I had never dreamed of, introducing me to people whose backgrounds could not be more different from mine. And he has taught me lessons on my travels. Whether a mansion in Atlanta or a tenement flat in Glasgow, a home is still a home. And when a woman who loves the Lord meets another who shares her faith, they meet as sisters. One of them may have great wealth and the other little of this world's goods, but they share the most precious things of all, the riches of the gospel. It was on that basis, and only on that basis, that I felt at home in Jenny's home in Coca Cola Mansion.

At a women's conference in Cyprus in 1994 I saw God breaking down barriers in a most moving way. Those present came from Israel, Egypt, Uzbekistan, Turkistan, Palestine, Iraq and Iran and they met together in fellowship and to learn from each other. I was there as part of the prayer team: politically it was thought to be necessary for there to be a covering of prayer. If ever a conference had the power to explode, this one had. Kay Arthur, from Precept Ministries in America, was the guest speaker and she took us through her book on John's Gospel. Each evening she ministered from Daniel and Revelation. The Israeli women felt moved to repent on behalf of their nation, especially to seek the forgiveness of the Egyptian and Palestinian delegates. When this was shared with the conference, one lady, whose country was at odds with Israel, was adamant in her refusal to accept their repentance. The prayer team spent a lot of time before the Lord, asking him to resolve the situation and to bring about a real spirit of unity. On the last day of conference we met round the Lord's Table to celebrate the breaking of bread. Just before the service was due to begin, the Israeli women stepped out to the front, their spokesman explaining that they wished to repent on behalf of their nation. The Lord's Spirit moved on those present. There was a brokenness and love which touched everyone's hearts. No-one was left out. Women expressed their national guilt and accepted forgiveness from those whose countries had been wronged. Even a woman from Northern Ireland asked forgiveness from the Scottish and English delegates. We were in a situation which was humanly speaking impossible, but the Lord broke it apart and poured out love and forgiveness. We knew we were in the presence of the living God.

Also that year I went to Moldova, but that deserves a chapter to itself. My travels, however, have not always taken me abroad. Prayer Chain is a lonely ministry. We receive a phone call full of information for prayer and in our own time bring this to the Lord. Sometimes we hear how he has answered, but often not.

Members can be remote from each other, and not all manage to meet even on a monthly basis. I have long felt a concern about this and over the years have tried to visit groups whenever I could. This has taken me to many parts of Scotland as well as to England and Wales. Having prayed that the ministry would stretch beyond Scotland, we invited Evelyn Christenson, on one of her visits across the Atlantic, to speak in several English cities. Christian Women Communicating Internationally joined with us and organised a meeting in London.

It was at this meeting in London that I first met Helen Rawlings, who joined us in Prayer Chain and became one of our leaders in the south of England. Helen had suffered with serious mental illnesses for many years. But, as a follower of the Lord Jesus, she knew that he alone could bring her the peace of mind she so longed for. During a time of prayer Helen heard God promise that he would heal her. Shortly afterwards she had a dream. In her dream she was shown a Victorian gothic structure. Helen was no stranger to delusions and fantasies; such was the nature of her illness, but she knew that this was neither. She knew that this had come from God. From that point on Helen noticed a change. She was beginning to take charge of her frightening and unruly thoughts, to capture them and take them in penitent prayer to Jesus. Helen was inspired and encouraged by Paul's words: 'We demolish arguments and every pretension that sets itself up against the knowledge of God, and we take captive every thought to make it obedient to Christ' (2 Cor. 10:5).

Over the following months, Helen began to know a peace of mind, and she continues to enjoy healing to this present day more than thirty years on. With her healing came a call to develop a ministry for others who suffered in mind and spirit, and she and her husband, John, saw develop as the Acorn Christian Healing Trust. Helen continued to look for her 'dream house'.

At the same time another Christian lady, Sister Mary Albert, was receiving her own vision from God. Mary Albert had been a member of St Dominic's Priory, Carisbrooke since just before the war. But the days at Carisbrooke were coming to an end. Mary Albert had the conviction to pray that it might not only remain a 'house of prayer', but that it might in some way serve the Body of Christ. So for twenty-five years, she and Helen prayed. Mary prayed that God would use Carisbrooke for his glory, and Helen for her 'dream house'. In 1993 both Helen and Mary rejoiced to see their visions being fulfilled as the newly founded Carisbrooke Priory Trust purchased the freehold of St Dominic's Priory together with more than ten acres of gardens and land.

Early on God gave the name 'The Open Door', and over the years many have come through the door. For some it has been the door out of the prison of troubled and fearful minds, others have found a way to restore broken relationships and many others have found the door to faith in Jesus. Christ is the foundation of the Priory, and that is made clear to all who come. All are welcome wherever they may be on their own spiritual journey. Helen is just one of the many women who became part of God's praying 'army'.

Wilma, who with her husband had returned from Belgium to work with Operation Mobilisation in Coventry, found a venue in Birmingham. As a result, Prayer Chain now has chain links in both England

and Wales. The Regional Leaders from all over the United Kingdom, eighteen in all, meet every three months in Glasgow. Nor has Ireland been forgotten. Evelyn did a seminar there too. Although it did not result in Prayer Chain extending in a formal way to the province, I have been over several times to speak at conferences and feel very much at home with the Christian women there.

The Lausanne Conference in 1996, this time held in Stuttgart, was one in which much valuable work was done in the realm of developing communications and evangelistic partnership. That was one of two visits to Europe that year. The second was to Budapest, where I had the privilege of attending another conference, for the first time accompanied by my Prayer Chain colleague, Rosalie Bisset. It was a great joy for me to share the experience with her. Women met together from all over Eastern Europe and I rejoiced in renewing friendships made in Vienna. Every conference has its highlights, and this one was no exception. The delegates from the West were invited to bring gifts to give to the Eastern European women. There was a room stacked full of lovely things! Those for whom they were brought were given bags and told to go into the room and choose any six things they wanted. One delegate from Bulgaria, where the economy was in a dire state, took a box of black tights to give to a friend who had lost her husband. There is a traditional period of mourning there and black tights were unavailable. Another woman picked up a teddy bear. 'Is that for your children?' someone asked. 'No,' she replied, 'it's for me. I've never had a teddy bear.'

Several testimonies were given at the conference, one of which I will never forget. Ana Veres from Romania told us about her family which had suffered terribly under communist rule. Her husband, a pastor, was twice poisoned by government officials yet had miraculously recovered. When their son was three years old, while giving a routine vaccination, the doctor injected a toxin. It caused his muscles to atrophy. At the time of the conference he was sixteen years old, weighed fifty pounds and was confined to a wheelchair. He was dying. The boy loved Jesus and, although I have not heard, I am sure he is now in heaven with his Saviour. When Ana was in hospital, another patient made it quite clear that she disliked her a great deal. Ana lived out her faith, trying to show love to her fellow patient who was about to have surgery. When the day came for the operation to be performed it had to be cancelled because the hospital ran out of gut to stitch the wound. Ana had her long hair cut off, and from the strands the surgeon was able to pick the longest and strongest and use them instead of gut, so enabling him to carry out the operation. Sacrifice takes on a new meaning in the light of such moving testimonies.

Through my visit to Jenny Millner in Atlanta I was invited along with Evelyn Christenson to speak at the launch of Heartprep, a prayer programme for the 1996 Olympic Games in Atlanta. Men and women of vision recognised the opportunity the Games presented to reach out with the gospel. Under the banner, *More than Gold*, they set out to show the uniqueness and the preciousness of Christ. The churches worked together, finding 3,000 Christian homes in which relatives of the athletes could stay during the Games.

Scriptures, books, magazines, videos, cassettes, CDs – all these were produced specially. Christians were trained to host sports clinics, perform street theatre, exhibit visual arts, take part in storytelling events, perform gospel music and much more besides. It was a terrific blessing to be part of such a concerted effort to reach out with the good news that Jesus is King.

I have travelled far and found much to thrill my soul. But I need only journey to Hamilton and the home of my friend Annie Black to remind myself that the gospel needs no frills. Annie and her husband had eleven children, all of whom were trained in the martial arts. Life for the Blacks was such that most of her boys have spent time in prison. It was while her son Philip was in Barlinnie Prison that he heard about Jesus and came to saving faith in him.

He wrote to Annie and told her about Jesus. Philip was never to be home again, he died as the result of a fall in prison. Among his possessions his mother found a Bible. One day when the district nurse called she found Annie curled up in a chair reading the Bible. 'What are you reading?' she asked. Annie looked up, 'I don't know,' she said, 'but I can't put it down.' The nurse offered to go with her to a mission which was being held at that time in Glasgow. Annie went a sinner and came home a saint. Life has never been easy for her, either before she was converted or afterwards. But Jesus is Lord of her humble home.

11

Peter's travels

If a man should come now to your door
Selling motorways, a rustle of money in his eyes
Do not buy his road, for it leads
To all our lost riches, our need of God.
(Kenneth Steven)

Mine was not the only well-stamped passport. The Lord had travel plans for Peter too. In 1992 he was invited to accompany Sammy Tippit, the American evangelist, on a mission to Moldova. Peter's brief was to speak to pastors on reaching prisoners, gypsies and businessmen with the gospel, three areas in which he had gained experience over the years. With God nothing goes to waste. We already had family connections in Eastern Europe. Our son, Graham, a Doctor of Theology and a lecturer at London School of Theology, the new name for London Bible College, had a remit from the Baptist Churches of Romania to train pastors in theology, from diploma standard right through to doctorates. This came about through one of the Romanian Baptist leaders, Joseph Tson, who had a burning desire to see Christian education, both theological and general, established in the former Iron Curtain states. He has seen his vision become reality with the establishment of Christian universities. En route to meet Sammy, Peter visited Romania.

That visit had a profound effect on Peter. Romania was in the throes of an economic disaster. But while despair was written across the faces of the people he saw on the streets, the Christians he met were so different. Poor as they were, there shone through their poverty a deep enthusiasm for the new life they had found in Jesus. The church of God, which had been sustained over seventy years of communism, had recently seen an ushering in of a brand new generation of believers. But there was an evil spirituality too as Satan struggled to fill the vacuum left by communism with the occult, pornography, cultic teaching and all other kinds of evil.

At the invitation of a gypsy pastor, Peter went to a ghetto outside the town of Oradea, a makeshift suburb housing 2,000 Hungarian gypsies. Carol, the pastor, had been a Christian for just two years, before that he was a hard fighting, drinking and dishonest gypsy. They stopped to listen to a little group of Christians singing. The words were translated for Peter. There, from the midst of abject poverty, rose these beautiful words:

> Jesus, take me as I am,
> I can come no other way.
> (D Bryant)

Peter was taken to a gypsy meeting place where he met between forty-five and fifty believers. Having been welcomed and introduced, Carol read Acts 10:30-35, where Cornelius speaks to the Apostle Peter. 'Four days ago I was in my house praying at this hour, at three in the afternoon. Suddenly a man in shining clothes stood before me and said, "Cornelius, God has heard your prayer and remembered your gifts to the poor. Send to Joppa for Simon who is called Peter. He is a guest in the home of Simon the tanner, who lives by the sea." So I sent for you immediately, and it was good of you to come. Now we are all here in the presence of God to listen to everything the Lord has commanded you to tell us' (Acts 10:30-33). It was with tears glinting in his eyes that Peter told me how, at that meeting, he wept as he listened to God's Word, feeling that if he were to touch the words in the Bible on his knee the ink might still be wet. So it was that God called my husband to a ministry in Eastern Europe.

The following year we were both invited to go back: Peter as part of Sammy Tippit's evangelistic team, and me to do a three-day women's conference with Tex, Sammy's wife. We had the privilege of staying on after the Americans left, and in that time we saw God move mightily among these people who for seventy years had been shackled by communism. Every morning we went with our interpreter to the train station in the capital city of Kishinev which milled with people laden with boxes of chickens, bags of potatoes and all the other goods they produced, as they headed off to sell them. After a time of singing, preaching and distributing the Scriptures, between thirty-five and fifty people responded and came to the Lord each morning, many with tears of repentance and joy streaming down their faces. Is it any wonder that Moldova found lodging in both our hearts?

The only equipment the believers there possessed to help them in the vast job of preaching the gospel to the whole of Moldova and beyond was one little hand-held microphone. Peter came home with a deep burden for their needs and set out to provide them with the best of equipment, a van fully fitted out with sleeping, cooking, eating and shower facilities as well as a public address system. With that they could go around Siberia, the Ukraine and Moldova sharing the good news of Jesus Christ. There were men there to do just that. Vladimir, who had one of the largest law firms in Moldova, gave up his business interests to serve God. Alexander Popov, the international violinist, a believer for just two and a half years, forfeited his career and went daily to the bus station, drawing a crowd by his beautiful playing, then preaching the gospel to the people. Peter set about raising the money, reckoning it would take £45,000. The fund had reached £13,000 when Vladimir phoned. 'How is the project going?' he asked. Peter brought him up to date. 'That's great,' was the response, 'but it will take you another two years to raise £45,000.' 'That's right,' Peter agreed. 'Do you realise how many souls will be in hell by that time?' asked our brother in the Lord. That shook us. The Lord's guidance was sought in prayer and his leading followed. Peter, who spent his working life among vehicles, knew many people in the trade. One of them shopped around, found a suitable vehicle, and fitted it with a public address system, spare tyres and parts. In August 1994 my husband drove it out to Moldova, accompanied by his friend, Charlie.

The journey took five days, during which the Lord confirmed the rightness of what they were doing in very wonderful ways. Having crossed by ferry from Hull to

Belgium they drove to Frankfurt to meet Vladimir. The plan was to drive through Germany, Austria, Hungary and Romania to Moldova. It was after midnight when they reached the German-Austrian border where they were refused entry because Vladimir had no visa. Faced with the choice of either returning to Berlin with the hope of getting a visa in the morning or trying a different route, they prayed and felt led to go by Czechoslovakia although this meant driving through the night by an unfamiliar route. Vladimir and Peter took turns at driving. It was a week later that my husband learned that his co-driver had only passed his driving test one month previously! Early in the morning they crossed into Czechoslovakia and drove on, not realising until mid-afternoon that they had fasted for twelve hours. Spotting a town in the far distance they headed for it and found a restaurant. After their meal Peter and Charlie waited outside for Vladimir.

Twenty minutes later they were still waiting. On going in, they saw their friend standing in a corner talking to the manageress who was in tears. Vladimir explained that she, Juliet, had just received Jesus as Saviour. The van jumped along the next few miles, such was the joy of its occupants. Their turnaround at the Austrian border had been Juliet's salvation.

They drove on into the dark, along an unlit country road. Suddenly, blinded by the headlights of a car coming out of a side road, Vladimir found himself careering towards a two-foot high stone wall. Despite his inexperience, he drew to a halt just a few inches from it. Characteristically for Eastern Europe, the police were there immediately. Peter and Charlie listened intently as Vladimir spoke and interpreted. The police wanted their documents. That wasn't a problem, they were in a briefcase in the van ... or so they thought. A thorough search did not find them. It was a little while before it dawned on them that they had left the briefcase in the restaurant. Fortunately Juliet had given her telephone number to Vladimir and a call to her, confirming that the case had been left and that she had taken it home with her, was enough to satisfy the police. The travellers did an about-turn. Before leaving, Vladimir drew up beside a young policeman standing apart from the others to confirm the route back. Soon the two were deep in conversation. Ten minutes later Vladimir turned to his waiting friends. 'Come on,' he said, 'let's get out.' In answer to the puzzled expressions that met him, he added, 'We are going to pray.' They did, and that young Czechoslovakian policeman accepted forgiveness and new life through Jesus. Rejoicing with the angels in heaven, Peter, Charlie and Vladimir drove on.

Half an hour into their return journey, a solitary policeman flagged them down. 'What's the problem?' Peter whispered, as Vladimir and the policeman talked. 'There's no problem,' they were assured, 'this man has just finished work and would like a lift home.' Peter, who was sitting behind Vladimir, moved over and the burly policeman sat beside him. Again their driver engaged the man in conversation. It was Peter who noticed a tear run down the hitch-hiker's face. Yet another soul was saved and the three travellers continued on their way, rejoicing and praising God as they passed unhampered through all the other frontiers. When Peter told me later of this remarkable journey, he explained that such was the spiritual fertility of people's hearts in Eastern Europe, it could only be explained by God turning on its head their seventy-years-long indoctrination in godlessness.

When Peter talks about the Moldovan people his eyes light up. They certainly did when he told me the following story. Ivan Belef, who pastored a large growing church and is now with the Lord spent several periods in prison for preaching the gospel during the communist regime. On one occasion he shared an overcrowded cell with thirteen other inmates. They lived under very severe restrictions, one of them being that the men were not allowed to play cards. But they did. From time to time an officer looking through the peephole on the cell door would see them playing and instigate a full-scale search. Every prisoner was removed from the cell and each searched thoroughly, as was the cell itself, pillows, mattresses, everything. But in all the searches no cards were ever found. I smiled when Peter told me how this was done. Among the prisoners were two professional pickpockets. When the first guard entered the cell one of them put the cards into his uniform pocket. And after all the men and the cell had been searched, when the last prisoner was returned and the door about to be shut, the cards were effortlessly removed from the guard's pocket, ready for the next game.

Could God ever use such criminal skill? In Moldova it seems he could ... and did. When Vladimir took several carloads of young Christians to distribute small New Testaments in a Moldovan town they discovered this was forbidden. Having prayed about it they were given a novel solution. Remembering that the town was notorious for its pickpockets, the young people put New Testaments into their pockets and handbags, exposing them very slightly. Every New Testament was taken! God grant they might also be read.

For years I had prayed that God would open a new door of ministry for Peter, especially as he neared retirement age. My prayers have been wonderfully answered. Having been the breadwinner all our married life, it was hard for my husband to contemplate giving up his job to spend more time on the work God was calling him to do. But, in answer to the clearest of calls, that is what he has done. Moldova Ministries was established as a Trust and registered as a charity. A Management Board was formed of a chairman, treasurer and secretary with Peter as Field Director. He still does some signwriting – that is necessary to pay the bills – but by far the bulk of his time is spent working for Moldova. He has been there seventy-eight times in the last twenty years and it still thrills me when I hear his accounts of these trips.

Moldova Ministries has developed along three lines: training pastors and other Christians in evangelism, work with orphans, and aid and evangelism, the last two going together. Training work is done through regular conferences on evangelism. These are not talking shops, rather they are full of theoretical teaching and practical application. Peter and the other trustees recognise that these two must always go together. Special subjects are tackled: reaching prisoners and gypsies being two of them. Moldovan Christians recognise that the spiritual hunger may not last. It is a window of opportunity too good to be missed.

The opening to work with orphans came through Christian friends in Moldova who spend much of their time caring for orphans in the city of Kishinev. Alexander and Irene Popov do this for love of the Lord and for love of his little ones. One day the Lord will say to them, and to all the other self-sacrificial believers presently giving their all for him, 'Come, you who are blessed by my Father; take your inheritance, the kingdom prepared for you since the creation of the world. For I was hungry and you gave me something to eat, I was thirsty and you gave me something to drink, I was a stranger and you invited me in, I needed clothes and you clothed me, I was sick and you looked after me, I was in prison and you came to visit me' (Matt. 25:34-36). And should they ask when they did all these things, as the people did in Jesus' story, he will surely answer them, 'I tell you the truth, whatever you did for one of the least of these brothers of mine, you did for me' (Matt. 25:40).

Peter felt an increasing responsibility to help provide for some of the orphanages and the children there. One little girl, Daria, had become a special project. She was born with a shortened leg, which was withered and dangled at half the length of the other. A bright child with a fine natural agility, Daria crawled and hopped her way around. Peter described her as a little sparrow with a broken wing. Her disability was probably the result of a radiation contamination to which her father, as a soldier, had been exposed. Arrangements were made to bring Daria to Scotland where she had surgery and was fitted with an artificial limb and was trained to walk. Moldova Ministries undertook to provide replacement limbs as she grew and to arrange education for her. With God's blessing, this enabled one little girl to rise above the abject poverty, which would have been her future as a disabled person in Moldova. Daria is now seventeen years old and she and her mother are believers in the Lord Jesus and worship in a church in the Ukraine.

When Peter and his colleague Jim became aware of the problems providing aid can cause, especially when only a few receive and others are left without, they decided to identify the needs of whole villages and try to meet them. For example, on one visit Peter attended the village funeral of a pastor. It rained and the mud was so deep that he left his shoes in it as he walked. All the others who attended wore cheap boots. None were adequately shod for the conditions that were far from unusual. Moldova Ministries bought Wellington boots in bulk quantities for everyone in that village, and perhaps in other villages too. They have the advantage of wearing well and being able to be passed from person to person without damaging feet. A month or two after humanitarian aid was delivered to a village, whether food or things such as boots, a team made up of Moldovan Christians would hold a gospel mission there and this inevitability led to Christian converts among the villagers. Later still Bible teaching conferences were arranged to help new Christians grow and to encourage them to become evangelists. Is it any wonder Peter's eyes light up when he talks about Moldova?

12

And so to pray

God moves in a mysterious way
His wonders to perform;
He plants His footsteps in the sea,
And rides upon the storm.
(William Cowper)

If I had to choose just one phrase to sum up my life's experience it would have to be 'an adventure with God'. From childhood till now, through good times and bad, in health and in sickness, that is how it has been. And I thank God that the theme which has run through the adventure has been the theme of prayer. Had I to put the story to music I would call it 'Variations on the Theme of Prayer'. And there have been variations. In this book I have tried to be honest about the times I have found prayer hard, even sometimes impossible. And it has moved me, as it always does, to share with others some of my most intimate times with my heavenly Father.

When I became a follower of Jesus Christ, I was instructed to 'go to church, read my Bible, AND PRAY'. I attended church and read my Bible, but I found it difficult to pray. It was only much later in my Christian life that I understood why. There is nothing the devil dreads as much as prayer! He is determined to keep us from praying, and when he does this he has won a victory in our lives. Satan loves to see us up to our eyes in work – provided we do not pray. He doesn't fear us reading God's Word – provided we do not pray. Someone has said, 'Satan laughs at our toiling, mocks at our wisdom, but trembles when we pray.'

That is why we find prayer difficult, because the devil doesn't want us to pray. How true that is. It is my experience that when I pray I so enjoy the fellowship I have with my Father that I could stay in prayer all day. But Satan does everything in his power to divert me from it. Because prayer affects the progress of his kingdom, he throws every trick in the book at us to keep us from this powerful discipline. However, it has been one of my greatest thrills to watch Satan defeated through the prayers of God's people. Because of the nature of its ministry, Prayer Chain has over the years met satanic opposition. But God has thwarted him over and over again and we continue to bring the needs of individuals, of our nation and of the world to the Lord. I see the present and increasing prayerful concern for our nation as a vast piece of machinery in which our ministry is, in God's economy, just a little cog. Along with countless individuals and the other praying ministries we are privileged to be used by God to stem evil and hasten the coming of his kingdom.

At the time of the South African elections I had an urgent call asking for prayer during the Johannesburg talks between Nelson Mandela, Chief Buthelezi, Lord Carrington and Henry Kissinger. We were asked to pray especially for Washington Okomo, a Christian from Kenya and a 'peace negotiator extraordinaire' with the United Nations, that he would be God's man in that crucial situation. The talks were taking place that very day. Two hours later, as many of our 1,000 members as could be contacted were praying. The television news later that evening was depressing. The talks had fallen apart and Carrington and Kissinger were on their way home. Buthelezi had left saying he would not participate in the elections and that there would be a bloodbath in South Africa.

A week later I had a phone call asking me to thank the women for their prayers. 'But the talks fell apart,' I protested. The story I was told thrilled me. The talks had indeed fallen apart; but when they did, Washington Okomo felt God prompting him to go to the airport and speak to Buthelezi, whom he knew, before he left. But when Okomo reached the airport the plane had already taken off. Despite that, he felt he should wait. Before long Buthelezi's plane developed engine trouble and was re-routed back, giving the men two hours together, by the end of which Buthelezi had agreed to take part in the peace negotiations. It was some time later I heard the end of the story. When the plane landed and was checked, nothing whatever could be found wrong with it. Kissinger, who had gone back to America, telephoned Okomo who had once studied under him. 'You were once my student,' he told him. 'Now you are my mentor.' Prayer Chain was just one little part of that wonderful scenario. We were asked to pray that Washington Okomo would be God's man in that situation. And he was. Someone has said, 'The power of prayer is no more or no less than the mighty power of God released through the life of a man or woman who stops being an obstacle of God. The power is God's alone.'

Accounts like that should inspire believers to be much in prayer. But not all prayers have obvious and immediate answers. The ultimate purpose of prayer, as of any other part of our lives as believers, is to glorify God. And we know from God's Word that he sometimes delays the answer to prayer in order that His name might be magnified.

Now a man named Lazarus was sick. He was from Bethany, the village of Mary and her sister Martha. This Mary, whose brother Lazarus now lay sick, was the same one who poured perfume on the Lord and wiped his feet with her hair. So the sisters sent word to Jesus, 'Lord, the one you love is sick.' When he heard this, Jesus said, 'This sickness will not end in death. No, it is for God's glory so that God's Son may be glorified through it.' Jesus loved Martha and her sister and Lazarus. Yet when he heard that Lazarus was sick, he stayed where he was two more days. Then he said to his disciples, 'Let us go back to Judea.' ... On his arrival, Jesus found that Lazarus had already been in the tomb for four days ... deeply moved, [he] came to the tomb. It was a cave with a stone laid across the entrance. 'Take away the stone,' he said. 'But, Lord,' said Martha, the sister of the dead man, 'by this time there is a bad odour, for he has been there four days.' Then Jesus said, 'Did I not tell you that if you believed, you would see the glory of God?' So they took away the stone. Then Jesus looked up and said, 'Father, I thank you that you have heard me. I knew that you always hear me, but I said this for the benefit of the people standing here, that they may believe that you sent me.' When he had said this, Jesus called in a loud voice, 'Lazarus, come out!' The dead man came out (John 11:1-7, 17, 38-44).

Bethany was not far from where Jesus was when he heard of Lazarus' illness. He could have been there much sooner. But had he done so, what would have been recorded in Scripture, if it had been recorded at all, would have been the healing of another sick man. Instead, we have a magnificent record of the Lord's power over death and the grave. For there was no doubting that Lazarus was dead; he had been buried four days. The Lord's delay in answering Martha and Mary's cry for help strengthened their faith and gave a most powerful demonstration of the glory of God.

It is not always easy to be patient when the Lord seems to delay answering our prayers. Lazarus' sisters must have found their time of waiting for the Lord very hard to bear. But their waiting was rewarded. Perhaps, like them, we carry much-loved members of our families to the Lord in prayer. We watch them living lives that give every indication that they are heading for a lost eternity. We know that the end of their soul-sickness is death and we plead for their lives. Yet the Lord delays in coming. This is a particular problem for those in any position of Christian leadership, not because they are intrinsically different from any other believer, but because their brothers and sisters in the faith don't seem to realise just that, thinking that manse families, evangelists' families, leaders' families are in some way different when, in fact, they have the same problems as everyone else. They, too, need to cling to the promises of God. 'This is what the LORD says: "A voice is heard in Ramah, mourning and great weeping, Rachel weeping for her children and refusing to be comforted, because her children are no more."

This is what the LORD says: "Restrain your voice from weeping and your eyes from tears, and your work will be rewarded," declares the LORD. "They will return from the land of the enemy. So there is hope for your future," declares the LORD. "Your children will return to their own land'" (Jer. 31:15-17). They, too, need to hang on in there. It is an exercise in patience. It is an exercise in humility. It is an exercise in faith. But may it be to the glory of God.

Over the years the Lord has laid a burden on my heart for the young people of our nation. I see them going along roads that have at best dead ends, and at worst death at their ends. Prayer Chain carries this concern too. Its members bear our society to God in prayer, recognising that among today's young people are tomorrow's leaders, the movers and shakers of the future.

God has chosen to do something that seems to us impossible, to affect the world through our prayers. Today God is looking for people whose eyes are open to the needs of the world and whose hearts break at what they see happening in it. He will take their broken hearts and turn them towards prayer. And who can say what will happen then? Prayer is indeed an adventure.

But it is not an adventure from which we retire at sixty-five, or which grows easier with the passage of years. My heart is so full when I think of the joy and privilege of working hand in hand with the holy God of the universe. The world is on God's heart, and it is in his heart to see his kingdom preached throughout it. In prayer God is giving us the opportunity to be part of his great plan. And it is God's plan, not ours, that matters. Why is it that evangelistic efforts often bring so few converts? Could it be that more time is spent planning campaigns than praying? We spend ten minutes in prayer and expect God to jump to attention and give hundreds of converts. The apostles spent days in prayer and God turned the world upside down. Jesus' early followers were not influential people with political power and friends in high places. Nor did they need to be. Taking their case to the highest throne of all, the throne of Almighty God, they went on in the strength that he supplied.

The church started with small beginnings but before long spread throughout the whole of the Roman Empire and beyond. What was its secret? Was it that the early church was made up of praying people? I believe it was.

Our prayers can go where our feet cannot. Prayer reaches behind the walls of Westminster, into lands where Islam holds sway, and right to the thick of the war zones of the world. Our prayers can affect the people in our street, getting behind closed front doors to where there are broken hearts searching for something, hungry hearts filling themselves with an abortive mix of alcohol, sex and drugs, anything to fill the space which they don't realise can only be filled by God. The challenge before us is enormous. The challenge before us is impossible, but we worship the God of the impossible. The Lord told Moses and the children of Israel to walk right through the Red Sea, and they did ... dry shod. If that is not impossible I don't know what is.

Nine-year-old Danny came bursting out of Sunday school like a wild stallion. His little eyes were darting in every direction looking for his dad. Then he caught his dad by his leg and yelled, 'Man, that story of Moses and all those people crossing the Red Sea was great.' His father looked down at him and smiled and asked him to tell him about it.

'Well,' said Danny, 'the Israelites got out of Egypt, but Pharaoh and his army chased after them. So the Jews ran as fast as they could until they got to the Red Sea. The Egyptian army was getting closer and closer, so Moses got on his walkie-talkie and called the Israeli Air Force to bomb the Egyptians, then they came to the Red Sea, Moses got on his walkie-talkie again and called the Israeli Navy and they built a pontoon bridge so the people could cross over. They made it!'

By now his dad was shocked. 'Is that what they taught you? Is that the way the story was told?'

'Well not exactly' Danny admitted. 'But if I told it to you the way they told it to us, you'd never believe it!' Yes he is the God of the impossible!

(As told by Charles Swindoll).

'God is also the God of the impregnable. Think of it, he pulled down the walls of the city of Jericho. God could have done that with a word but he chose to do it through his people. Instructing them to circle the walls daily for a week, he waited as they did so. Only on the seventh day, as they obeyed him further, did the walls fall. God chose to work through the obedience of his people. He still does. The Bible teaches, 'pray continually' (1 Thess. 5:17). 'Do not be anxious about anything, but in everything, by prayer and petition, with thanksgiving, present your requests to God. And the peace of God, which transcends all understanding, will guard your hearts and your minds in Christ Jesus' (Phil. 4:6-7).

'That is the obedience to which we are called. And I have proved over and over again the promise which accompanies it. Prayer Chain, by its very nature, has resulted in many harrowing calls. People at the end of their tether have phoned and poured out their hearts to me. I have found myself in counselling situations, which I could share with nobody but the Lord. Although they would find their way through the chain, they did so in general terms and without their dreadful details. Had I carried these burdens away from my place of prayer they would have weighed me down and the cumulative effect would have been unbearable. But God has kept his promise. Having taken these situations to him he has guarded my heart and mind. The strange thing is that I forget the lurid details and I thank God for that.

'How precious is prayer but how often the business of prayer is interrupted by the busyness of life. It is so easy to fool ourselves into thinking that to be busy is to do God's will. Had the Israelites outside Jericho spent their days drawing up plans, discussing strategies, worrying and fretting, would the walls have come down any sooner? Of course not. So often we try to push God's hand. We make plans for him without as much as consulting him about them. We try to organise him, and organise him out of business so far as bearing any fruit in our lives is concerned. Someone has said, 'When we depend on organisation we get what organisation can do. When we depend on education we get what education can do. When we depend on God we get what God can do.' We fall prey to all the wiles of Satan, forgetting that our place is to be still before the Lord. He will lead when the time comes to move. He will prompt when the time comes to act. And while moving and acting are both important, what is most important of all is our relationship with Christ. Prayer is not merely a religious exercise that Christians perform. Neither is it seeking a handout from God. Prayer is seeking to know God.'

Christianity is not a religion so much as a relationship. And as relationships only deepen when people spend time together, we need to ask ourselves at the end of each day how much time we have spent with our Lord.

William Cowper put it beautifully:

O for a closer walk with God,
A calm and heavenly frame,
A light to shine upon the road
That leads me to the Lamb!

The dearest idol I have known,
Whate'er that idol be,
Help me to tear it from Thy throne,
And worship only Thee.

So shall my walk be close with God,
Calm and serene my frame;
So purer light shall mark the road
That leads me to the Lamb.

When I was in St Thomas's Hospital in a coma, I could so easily have stepped through a door and been with the Lord. I wanted to go but was told to go back. Go back to what? What did it mean? I wonder if, when the Apostle Peter denied the Lord, he thought about going back to that day on the Mount of Transfiguration when he, along with James and John, saw the Lord in all his glory. Or Paul, when he went through times of discouragement, would like to have gone back to that day on the Damascus road, when he encountered the risen Lord.

Then there is Moses, when he came down from the mountain after receiving the Law and saw the people worshipping a golden calf, and heard the grumbling of the people. Did he think back to that day in the desert when he was confronted by the burning bush, or when he saw the glory of God? What was on God's heart for me to go back to? Have you wandered from the Lord? Is God asking you to go back? Back to the decision you once made to Jesus Christ? Back to Calvary, to once again see God's love for you in action!

Three times it seemed I was slipping away and my family was sent for. The Scripture God gave Peter and our three other friends was this, 'Wake up! Strengthen what remains and is about to die, for I have not found your deeds complete in the sight of my God.' For two years I did not know what that meant. I was not about to die. My work was to continue. To what did it refer?

I struggled with this question until one evening after I had been speaking, Peter remarked, 'You said something tonight I've never heard you say before, *"the dying discipline of prayer"*. My spirit responded immediately; that's it! Prayer is a dying discipline for many. My mind went back to the days when I was a young woman, spending evenings in prayer, when our church prayer meetings were packed and full of excitement, when we prayed and expected God to answer. I compared those days with the prayer meetings today in many churches when the prayers are so introvert, without vision, expectancy or waiting on God. We come into the presence of a holy, holy, holy God with unclean hands, impure hearts and carrying our shopping lists with us. No wonder our prayer meetings are often dull and uninspiring!

When I was invited to lead a women's conference on prayer in Moldova I struggled because, when these women pray, there is power released from heaven. I told them I wanted to put them in my suitcase and bring them all back to the UK to show what praying in the Spirit (not in tongues) is really like. They pray with broken repentant hearts. And they could be in prayer for hours, worshipping God in prayer, making intercession for others and expecting God to answer. Oh to see that kind of praying here in the West.

We talk about prayer and read about prayer but do we really believe in the power of prayer? Samuel Chadwick says, 'The world will never believe in a religion in which there is no power. A rationalised faith, a socialised church, a moralised gospel may gain applause but they awaken no conviction and gain no converts.' My unfinished work was the work of Prayer Chain, the work of encouraging women to be practical prayers.

And if God can take and use me, an ordinary housewife from Glasgow, he can do the same for you. How wonderful it will be in glory for ordinary people like you and me if we find ourselves standing beside someone who turns to us and says, 'I'm here because you prayed for me.'

13

Vital links

You can count how many seeds are in an apple
But you cannot count how many apples are in a seed.
(Karen Jensen)

Have you ever looked back over your life and thought about the people you have met and known who have made an impact on your life, those who have been links to lead you on to an experience which has influenced you in either a personal or spiritual way? This story taken from *Word for Today* expresses it beautifully.

'In 1858, a Boston Sunday School teacher named Kimball began visiting one of his students at the shoe shop where he worked as a clerk. Eventually he led him to Christ. That student's name was D. L. Moody. Twenty-one years later, Moody, now an evangelist, visited London and a great spiritual awakening took place. F.B. Meyer, a local pastor, went to hear Moody and his life was transformed. Later Meyer went to America to preach and in one of his meetings a student named J. Wilbur Chapman got saved. Chapman became active in the YMCA, where he met and discipled, a former baseball player called Billy Sunday. Sunday became a great revivalist and, in one of his crusades in Charlotte, a group of businessmen came to Christ. A year later, they decided that their city needed another crusade, so they invited Mordecai Hamm to be their speaker. Three weeks later Hamm left town, discouraged because he'd only had one convert – a twelve-year-old boy called Billy Graham.'

That one Sunday school teacher quite unknowingly started a chain of vital links, which led to the conversion of God's man, who has been wonderfully used by God to bring many to the person who changed their lives. Just one person can make all the difference. I want to be that person. You can be too!

I thank God for the many vital links I have met who have made an impact on my life, as I led Prayer Chain Ministry for twenty-five years. In a previous chapter I mentioned my privileged involvement with what was originally Concern for Scotland (later Evangelical Alliance). I thank God for the strong leadership of the Rev. Fergus MacDonald who, along with the Rev. David Anderson and Rev. Robert McGhee, (both now with the Lord), and other godly men and women, made up the delegation of twenty-five that went to the Lausanne Congress in Manila in 1989.

At the Lausanne Congress, I met two wonderful servants of God, Sammy and Tex Tippit. Sammy and Tex came to the prayer workshop I led and I learned that Sammy was holding prayer seminars for the week of the Congress. I went to each one and was thrilled to see the anointing of God on this young man. A few years later Sammy was the conference speaker at the Faith Mission in Edinburgh. I invited him to be our guest speaker at the Prayer Chain Conference. When I was prayer co-coordinator for the 1991 Billy Graham Mission in Glasgow, I again invited Sammy to speak at some prayer rallies held before the mission. Sammy and Peter became friends and in 1992 Sammy invited Peter to go with him on mission to Moldova. It was there Peter fell in love with that little country and Moldova Ministries was born. VITAL LINKS!

I am astounded at God's unfolding plans for our lives. I'm sure Esther, whose story is told in the book of Esther, was a little nobody in the eyes of those around her, but not in the eyes of God. She never dreamt that she should one day be Queen of Persia. Nor did I ever dream that I would meet and spend time with such wonderful men and women of God. The story of Esther is a good example of what it means to be a vital link for the kingdom of God. Esther was chosen, prepared for royalty, commissioned and 'brought to the kingdom for such a time as this'. She was God's chosen link to fulfil God's purposes and plans for the nation of Israel. God's Name is never mentioned in this book, **but God** was working out his will and preparing her for her role as queen. God too has chosen us. 'For he chose us in him before the creation of the world to be holy and blameless in his sight' (Eph. 1:4).

It is my prayers that, no matter where you may be in your Christian walk with God, you will understand that you are important to God, and that the people and circumstances in and around your life are under his control. You may feel in a dark place right now; you may be suffering through illness, depression, anxiety about your family. You may be discouraged and feel that you are alone and God is at a distance. **BUT GOD** is not far from you. He has promised never to leave you or forsake you.

I have found that I have learned more about God in the valleys than in my mountaintop experiences. I love this Johnny Cash song.

> I've had tears and sorrows; I've had questions for
> tomorrow
> There've been times I didn't know right from wrong.
> But in every situation God gave blessed consolation
> That my trials only came to make me strong.

> Through it all, through it all, I've learned to trust in
> Jesus
> I've learned to trust in God.
> Through it all, through it all
> I've learned to depend upon His Word.

The interesting thing is that I couldn't sing this song with real conviction until after my brain hemorrhage.

God's networking in bringing vital links into my life continued when the Prayer Chain Committee invited Evelyn Christenson to Scotland to be guest speaker at our Prayer Chain Conference in 1990. Three years later I was at an AD2000 Conference in Lizst in Austria where I met Pam Johnson. Pam worked for Evangelical Ministries in Belfast, Northern Ireland, and was Chairwoman of Focusfest, an annual weekend event which brought 4,000 women from all denominations across Ireland to pray and learn together. When Pam heard that Evelyn was coming to Scotland she invited her to be the guest speaker at Focusfest. Little did I know that I was included in the programme and had my first experience of speaking to so many people.

Evangelical Ministries also cared for those who had lost their husbands. Minus One was mainly led by widows who cared for those recently bereaved. Having been through the trauma themselves they were the best people to help others. It was my privilege to speak at several of their weekend conferences and share the Word of God.

As a result of my visits to Focusfest God began to burden my heart to see something similar in Scotland. I knew the potential that Christian women could reach beyond making tray-bakes and offering hospitality. To understand what God wanted me to do to make a difference in my community, I began to meet every week with four other friends from different denominations to seek Gods' plan for us and what we could do to make a difference in South Ayrshire. We prayed for guidance for a number of months and God gave an answer. I knew a friend, another link in Inverness, who had been burdened to see a Crisis Pregnancy Centre established in her area. I invited Catherine to come and share with women from the local churches in South Ayrshire. A number of women came and Catherine shared how God had enabled women at the centre to help those who were struggling with possible abortions. The vision was caught by a few attending the meeting and a Crisis Pregnancy Centre was opened in February 2003 and has had over 800 contacts, including 200 by secure broadband online counselling. Twenty-five people have been trained as advisors and twelve trained as post-abortion counsellors. Referrals for post-abortion counselling come from the National Health Service. The person who headed up the Centre was also a leader in Prayer Chain. Mary has surrounded the Centre with prayer and God has blessed the work. This was a great encouragement to our little prayer group.

Women from many denominations met regularly to implement the vision of Scotfest, which was to encourage women from every denomination in Scotland to work together to reach out to family, neighbours and friends who are hurting and can find no answer to life's problems, and to tell them that they matter to God.

We found encouragement from a poignant image from Loren Eisley's book *The Star Thrower*. Picture a beach covered in thousands of starfish that have been washed up high by the tide and are dying on the sand. A little boy is patiently throwing them one by one back into the sea. He is asked why on earth he is bothering when clearly there are so many it's not going to make a difference. 'Well if I don't they'll die.' The little boy picked up another starfish, threw it back into the ocean and said, 'It's going to make a difference to this one.' So the theme of Scotfest became 'People matter to God. Do they matter to you?' Yes, we can make a difference.

This story taken from *Word for Today* shows what God can do with someone thrown on a garbage heap!

Benson Idahosa died a few years ago. Even though he was just 59, his friend Bishop Paulk said at his funeral, 'Benson had finished his course!' And what a course it was! He began his life as an abandoned baby on a garbage heap in Benin City, Nigeria. But the Bible says, 'When my father and mother forsake me, then the LORD will take me up' (Ps. 27:10, KJV). God had plans for Benson. During his amazing life he built the first Christian University in Africa, a hospital, a school and an orphanage for children just like him who had been abandoned. Besides building a cathedral for his congregation of 25,000 people, he became a bishop to 6,000 other pastors worldwide.

So what do we learn from a man like this? First, your future is not determined by your past! Benson turned every painful experience into wisdom and compassion and made this world a better place for all of us. The power that brought healing to him was the message he carried to others. Here was his life's theme: 'The Spirit of the LORD is upon me, because he has anointed me to preach the Gospel to the poor; he has sent me to heal the brokenhearted, to preach deliverance to the captives and recovering of sight to the blind, to set at liberty them that are bruised.' (Luke 4:18, KJV).

A team of us worked together for several years and then on 3rd June 2000 in the SECC Glasgow, Anne Graham Lotz, Dr Billy Graham's daughter, addressed a gathering of 2,200 women from all over Scotland.

The following year, Kay Arthur of Precept Ministries USA was our guest speaker in the Armadillo, Glasgow to which 1,800 women came, again from all over Scotland. Both of these godly women brought God's Word alive and many were blessed and lives were changed. Looking back over the years, I stand in awe at the grace of God, who brought such women of God into my life. Evelyn Christenson, who was used to introduce Prayer Chain, for thirty years has been standing in the gap for our nation. Kay Arthur has given me a thirst for the Word of God, and Anne Graham Lotz has encouraged me by her gentle faith and zeal for God.

God opened doors for me to speak and share Scotfest around Central Scotland and I believe that he touched some lives. In certain churches, where there was no prayer meeting, through the vision of Scotfest prayer meetings were started. The time came when I felt that I should withdraw from the committee and left Scotfest, but not the burden or vision. Sadly Scotfest did not continue for long. It may be that this was not God's time for Scotfest and I ran ahead of the Lord, but the vision still remains with me and my prayer is that God will raise up a woman or women to 'look on the harvest fields which are white and ready for harvest' and see the potential.

14

On to Africa

I was hungry and you gave me food;
I was thirsty and you gave me drink;
I was a stranger and you took me in;
I was naked and you clothed me;
I was sick and you visited me.
(Matt. 25:35-36, KJV)

When I was a teenager I loved reading books written by missionaries, Isobel Kuhn was one of my favourites. Lost in the adventures and the excitement of reading what God had done in her life, I could imagine being a missionary and thought only about the excitement of what it might be like. The church to which I belonged supported a number of missionaries and held conferences to which several who were home on furlough came and shared their experiences; I loved to hear their stories. The ones who impressed me most were those who did not hark back to when they were 'called' to the mission field, but those who could tell of what God was doing NOW.

However, it seemed that God was not going to answer my desire, as his plan for me was to be a wife, mother and housewife. Then, in 2000, I was invited to go to Uganda. On my first of three visits I was invited by the Mother's Union, a branch of the Ugandan Anglican Church, to speak to the Mother's Unions in and around Kampala.

Again God's plans were being worked out through 'Vital Links'. When I spoke at the first Minus One Conference in Northern Ireland, I met a lady who had been a missionary in Africa, but was now a business-woman in Northern Ireland. Valerie is a vital link in Focusfest and on fire for God. She and another link, Sharon, had been to Uganda, and it was through them the invitation came. I travelled with Valerie, Sharon, and my friend and colleague Ophelia, who comes from Ghana.

As soon as you leave the air-conditioning of the plane, you are hit with a blast of hot air, like the opening of an oven door! Africa! I was so glad Ophelia was with me as she was a tremendous help to me culturally. I recall one day arriving at a village to speak. As soon as I got out of the car one of the Ugandan ladies grabbed my handbag. I immediately grabbed it back from her, until Ophelia explained that this was their way of being kind, by carrying my bag!

For most of us living in the West we have no idea of the abject poverty in the Third World. It is a shock to see those who have absolutely nothing, heartbreaking to see little children with rags for clothes and no shoes on. Having no toys, they play with empty bottles or old tyres. In the villages families live in shacks put together with anything they can find. Even in homes with dirt floors and no lighting, the children, who know no better, are smiling and happy.

My friends Valerie and Sharon saw the great need to help young girls who had been raped. Many such are put out on the streets and are vulnerable and prey to all sorts of trouble. A ministry called Waakisa Ministries was born of God. I was invited to join the Northern Ireland Board and have had the privilege of working with men and women who have a BIG heart for these young women.

Ground was purchased in 2002 at Kitala just outside Entebbe, and there is now a compound which houses an education unit, a guest house which sleeps sixteen. There is also a Crisis Pregnancy Centre, accommodation for the girls and staff and a kitchen. At present we are building a halfway house for girls and their babies who cannot go back to their homes. We have a cow and her calf and pigs. The compound is securely guarded night and day. At the time of writing we have twenty-one girls and eleven babies in residence.

Each week a report is sent to Sharon from our Ugandan Administrator, the following is one such report.

HOME CARE

We had quite a number of deliveries in this month namely: Barbara delivered a baby boy normally on 21ˢᵗ June 2010 and was discharged on 22 / 6/ 2010, the baby weighed 3.3kgs and named Godfrey. Winnie was admitted in hospital on 24/6/2010 when she was in labor pains and she delivered on the 26ᵗʰ.

In addition, a lot of our girls and their babies have been sick and Marjory suffering from cough and flu. However there are other diseases other than cough and flu that have attacked the girls for example Nakuya Barbara is suffering from typhoid and on treatment although the Doctor advised us to stop Barbara from breast feeding her baby so at the moment the baby is taking milk.

Home has discharged two girls that is Annet and Christine and by the time these girls left our centre, they were healthy with the babies.

This period we have admitted five girls namely Joan on 4th. This girl was in a certain clinic trying to carry out an abortion due to the fear she had for her father to know yet he was paying school fees Milly from Wakiso district was admitted on the 10th she was still schooling and when she got pregnant her step father did not want to see her any more. Harriet from Kayunga district was a student and the fellow student responsible denied the reality.

Joan from Kayunga district was in her senior four vacation and got pregnant but the man responsible disappeared and is no where to be seen.

Lastly Jackline was admitted on 21st from an island was raped by a guardian's son and when the guardian discovered that she was pregnant he straight away threw her out of his home.

One of our girls Annet accepted Jesus Christ as her personal savior on 30th. Further more, Annet (maama Patrick) and Hawa (Maama Alpha) have been studying confirmation and were confirmed so now they are full Christians.

The girls are taught life-skills, such as cooking, housekeeping, sewing, tailoring and crafts, so that when they go back to their villages they will be able to support, not only their baby, but also their whole family. When a girl shows ability in sewing she is given a treadle sewing machine when she leaves the centre. Most of the girls have to leave school and this upsets her parents because education has to be paid for. We have a teacher who educates them while they are with us and they are also taught God's Word to equip them for the future.

I thank God for the wonderful opportunity he has given me at my age to be a very small part of this wonderful ministry. There is no retirement in the service of the Lord Jesus Christ. We get a retread, as our 'outer man' grows older and weaker, our 'inner man' gets stronger by the enabling power of the Holy Spirit. Jesus said, 'My grace is sufficient for you, for my power is made perfect in weakness.'

When a car is parked, it is motionless. What makes it work? The engine does, but it needs a driver to put it into gear and it needs fuel in the tank. It doesn't matter how old the car is, or whatever state the car is in, it is useless without fuel and driver. So too in our Christian lives, we need Christ and his power in us to motivate us and enable us to live powerful Christian lives. So no matter what age you are, God can still use you to fulfil his purposes. Go for it!

15

Moldova Ministries

Blessed are those
who hunger and thirst for righteousness,
for they will be filled.
(Matt. 5:6)

As I write this chapter in April 2010, a volcanic eruption has taken place in Iceland, exploding enormous clouds of black ash into the atmosphere. This is causing widespread chaos in the aircraft industry across Europe, with disruption to travellers hoping to return to Europe from every other part of the world.

The Lord Jesus during his earthly ministry reminded his hearers that 'Not one sparrow falls to the ground, but its heavenly Father knows.'

How thankful we should be that the God in whom we trust is interested in the smallest things in his creation. Among the nations of the world, the little independent State of Moldova has little intrigue or influence commercially. Presently it remains the poorest country in Eastern Europe. But despite its shattered economy the average Moldovan demonstrates a high level of intelligence. More importantly, from Peter's personal view, the Lord's people are not retarded by their circumstances, but rather are an advancing church with great vision, unhindered by complacency. This 'first love' enthusiasm which Peter encounters on each visit over the past nineteen years since he first set foot in Moldova, fuels his own vision and enthusiasm for the gospel.

Earlier comments in the book regarding Moldova stated the importance of humanitarian aid. Since those early years, after reviewing costs, outlays, etc., the board of Moldova Ministries (M.M.) felt that this programme had fulfilled its purpose. Today we purchase material supplies in Moldova, thus supporting the local economy and decreasing our financial outlay. By God's grace six churches have been built, mostly in outlying villages, and pastors are ordained and supported by M.M.

The needs of the poorest children in Moldova has not missed God's glance. Through an excellent dedicated team from M.M.'s base church in Ciocana, a large region of the capital city Chisinau, a vital work is done among deprived children. This ministry is called H&H (Hands and Hearts). Many of those boys and girls, when first received at H&H, have to be deloused, cleaned and clothed. The background and family circumstances of each child is established, all with a view to helping them best. Many are non-attendees at school; some are detached from their families. All receive wholehearted kindness. For most this is their first experience of unconditional love.

Some of the leaders are married with families yet willingly make space in their lives for such boys and girls. One of the valued leaders is Tanya who was herself a street child. At the age of fourteen a team member who had been a 'woman of the streets' introduced her to H&H. Tanya was traumatised on her arrival. Her family life was difficult. In her tender years she knew what it was to be sexually abused and to live under that constant possibility at home. For two years prior to her introduction to H&H, Tanya and another girl slept up trees. Today, as a born-again believer and a much respected member of her church, she serves these children with a heart and mind that feels their pain totally. One of the children, when asked what she would like to be when she grew up replied, 'I want to be like Tanya.' God has gifted Tanya with the ability to see the possibilities in the most deprived child.

I was invited to hold a Day Conference in Bethany Church, and something I said was used by God to touch a woman called Helena, who has a severely disabled child. She immediately saw a need for fellowship and support for others with disabled children. M.M. learned of her desire and they now support My Child is My Blessing, a ministry working from Bethany Baptist Church at Ciocana.

When Peter visited Moldova in 2009 he was invited to speak at the Sunday morning service and joining him were several disabled young people. One fourteen-year-old boy with cerebral palsy sang 'Holy, Holy, Holy' first in Russian and then in Hebrew. Following him, a nine-year-old girl, also severely disabled, recited the first chapter of Matthew's Gospel. Others recited poems and a group of parents sang as a sextet. Finally a sixteen-year-old boy in a wheelchair recited a poem, the theme being 'Do not ask why God made me like this; you will only destroy your faith.' It is possible no-one remembers what Peter preached that morning, but I'm sure that they will never forget the powerful message from these disabled children and their parents. My Child is My Blessing is a powerful, beautiful and essential Ministry, which perhaps brings a twinkle of delight to the eye of God.

In the Ciocana region of Chisinau there is a population of 200,000, of whom 22,000 are elderly. The elderly of Moldova have a bad deal when it comes to social and health care. Until recent years pension payments were irregular, some waiting a year for payment. Peter tells of meeting elderly villagers appealing for help with tears in their eyes. Such things are not common now, but what they do receive is still no relief from very frugal living. From each of the churches M.M. has planted or built come stories of present and past hardships experienced by the elderly. Three days each week at Bethany Church, fifty to sixty elderly people receive generous nourishing meals and also takeaway meals for ill or housebound spouses. These meals are a much-appreciated lifeline.

The life stories of some of these dear people are very moving. Some were doctors, nurses, school teachers, loyal factory workers, farm workers, vets, museum curators, etc. Any one of them can tell of cruel periods in their lives. Some tell of famines when dead bodies in the streets were a common sight. Many recall eating grass and leaves, anything to survive starvation. When some had no shoes, they cut rubber tyres in the shape of feet and tied them on with string. One former senior nurse tells how she had only one dress to wear. Her mother washed it at night in the hope of having it dry and ready for the next morning.

It was on a 2009 visit to an apartment in one of the many fourteen-storey buildings, where a common kitchen and toilet served eighteen families, that Peter met Lydia and Sergie, both seventy-six years old. Six years previously Sergie suffered a stroke and was paralysed. He needed constant care from his loving wife. Their only son died of a heart attack. In her distress Lydia questioned why her husband, who is an enormous burden to her, was left and her son was taken. However, she continues caring and loving Sergie. Her only respite is when a kind neighbour sits with him for two hours to allow Lydia to enjoy company and have her meal at Bethany. She brings her husband a packed meal and regards this kindness as a blessing from God. It is very sad to imagine that this couple have no social help or visiting nurse. A doctor is available only if they are able to pay his attendance fee.

John 6:5 describes the Lord Jesus seeing a great multitude of people, more than 5,000, and all hungry. His compassionate look was followed by action, which resulted in total satisfaction for the entire crowds of followers. M.M. is thankful for the dedicated pastors who look here and there for needs and are ready and eager to serve those for whom such welfare as there is in Moldova has failed. These pastors are truly biblical shepherds with a genuine sensitiveness of heart to the real spiritual needs of their flocks.

I have been blessed by Peter's accounts of the spiritual discipline of pastors when, for example, they have fasted for one week, not for domestic or personal needs, but to gain a deeper understanding of God. Entire congregations sometimes set aside a Sunday for fasting and praying for the spiritual needs of their surrounding communities. These meaningful times take place frequently as spiritual leaders wait on the Lord's leading. Peter and I count it a gift from the Lord to be privileged to serve him among such chosen people.

16

Commitment

It was character that got us out of bed,
commitment that moved us into action,
and discipline that enabled us to follow through.
(Zig Ziglar)

You may have heard the story of the chicken and the pig. The two were travelling along a country road when they noticed an announcement on the bulletin board of a little country church. The sign read, 'Ham and eggs breakfast this Sunday at 7:30 am. All are invited.' The pig turned to the chicken and said, 'Will you look at that! That for you is no more than a days work, but for me its total commitment! Commitment is costly!'

In 1858 a small frail lad was born to a rich family in New York. Along with feeble eyesight, he suffered from asthma, so bad that he sometimes couldn't blow out the bedside candle, nevertheless he became one of the most powerful people of his time. At eleven or twelve years of age Theodore Roosevelt's father told him that a good mind alone would not ensure success, he must build himself a powerful new body to match it. Theodore spent thousands of hours lifting weights and rattling a punching bag. It's little wonder he rose like a rocket in the world of politics.

Elected to the New York Legislature at twenty-three, candidate for mayor at twenty-eight, he was the US Civil Service Commissioner under two Presidents; President of the Police Commision of New York; national hero of the Tough Riders in the Spanish American war at forty; then in just three busy years, Governor of New York, Vice-President, then President.

In 1905 Teddy Roosevelt received the Nobel Peace Prize for his efforts in helping to end the Russo-Japanese war. At five feet nine inches, Roosevelt, a small man, was made large through commitment (by Geoffrey C. Wad, *Success Magazine*).

We live in a time when commitment is not the most popular word in our vocabulary. Many find it hard to make a commitment in marriage. Employers cannot make a commitment that there will be enough work. We are not even committed to things we own as we throw them away rather than fix them. It seems that commitment to anything is painful, uncomfortable, and makes too much of a demand on our time and resources.

Commitment is the willingness to do whatever it takes; it is a heartfelt promise to yourself from which you refuse to back down. There's a difference between interest and commitment. When you are interested in doing something, you do it only when it is convenient. When you are committed you accept no excuses – only results. I think of my father, who for forty years held the position of treasurer in the church we attended. I have many memories of him spending hours at home preparing the church accounts. Such standards of integrity and commitment were not uncommon in those past times. Perhaps those of yesteryear had a true perception of the brevity of time and the great honour of being a servant of Jesus Christ. Thank God for the many today who fulfil their commitment to the Lord's work with a willing heart, not counting the cost.

When God called me to lead the Telephone Prayer Chain Ministry in 1981, I knew that this was a calling from him. Although there were times when I struggled, I knew I had made a commitment which brought responsibility. Eddie Askew in his book *A Silence and a Shouting* has this to say about commitment: 'Much of the stress in our lives comes from our flight from the totality of commitment. We run from responsibilities we don't want to accept. We run from confrontation because we lack the courage to look at ourselves in the clear light of God's presence. We run because total commitment demands more change in our lives than we have the courage for. Yet running, we never arrive; we find no hiding place, nowhere is safe from God; and the only way to come to terms with the tension of God's presence is acceptance.'

With the responsibility came many wonderful opportunities, some of which I have already mentioned. Looking back over the past years, especially the years leading Prayer Chain, I'm eternally thankful to God for the privilege of being a servant in the wonderful ministry he birthed almost thirty years ago. Had I never made a commitment, I would have been so much the poorer in every way. It must be very sad to look back over a lifetime and recall missed opportunities, as the following story shows.

A man once went with a friend for a ride in the country. They drove off the main road and through an orange grove to a mostly uninhabited piece of land. Walter stopped the car and began to describe vividly the things he was going to build on the land. He wanted his friend Arthur to buy some of the acreage surrounding his project. Walter explained to his friend, 'I can handle the main project myself. It will take all my money, but I want you to have first chance at this surrounding acreage, because in the next five years it will increase in value several times.' Arthur thought to himself, 'Who in the world is going to drive 25 miles for this crazy project?' He mumbled something about a tight money situation and promised to look into the deal later. 'Later will be too late,' Walter cautioned. 'You'd better move on it now.' Arthur failed, however, to act. So it was Arthur Linkletter turned down the opportunity to buy the land that surrounded what became Disneyland, the land his friend Walt Disney tried to talk him in to purchasing.

When I was ill in London, and thought I might die or be incapacitated, I made a vow to God that, if he spared me, I would do whatever he asked until he took me home.

Since that time, only through God's amazing powerful grace, I have endeavoured to keep my vow. 'And having said goodbye to the ordinary I have endeavoured to march on beyond the extraordinary.' 'I strain to reach the end of the race and receive the prize for which God is calling us up to heaven because of what Christ Jesus did for us' (Phil. 3:14 TLB).

I stepped down from the leadership of the Prayer Chain in 2006, which was not without great sadness as it was hard to let go. For twenty-five years this ministry had held my heart and I had come to love dearly those whom God had brought around me. When God's Holy Spirit breathes life into a ministry he ensures that leadership is in his hands. I thank God that Prayer Chain did not die when I stepped down. In fact, God is adding to this ministry and he will faithfully equip those, who by his grace, will take it forward for as long as it is in his will. It is also encouraging that many of the women who have been involved have now started prayer chains within their own churches. Like a stone thrown into a pool, the ripples are widespread.

But God still had work for me to do. You do not retire in the Lord's work; you get a retread and continue to be available. I help Peter with the administration for Moldova Ministries and I continue to be involved in Uganda. Our five grandchildren, Gavin, Katie and Flora, are very precious to us and we are available to care for our two youngest, Olivia and Niamh, who live close to us in Prestwick. I have also made space to take up embroidery again, a hobby that I love.

Looking back over the writings in this book, I suppose my life could be likened to a tapestry, or embroidered picture which is not yet complete. The underside of a good tapestry looks as good as the upper side, but I'm sorry to say that my work does not always reach that standard! To enhance the gold, silver and bright hues, there have to be some dark threads. I can recall a few of these when I struggled to be real, and God had to take me through the refiner's fire to teach me to pray. I also can relate to the black threads of illnesses, especially when God laid me aside in London with a brain haemorrhage. **But God:** how I love these two words. They give the joy and comfort of knowing that even when the dark threads are woven through our tapestry, God is in control.

Then there are the gold and silver threads, the highlights of the tapestry. How thankful I am that these threads stand out, like my fifty-six years of marriage to Peter and for the joy and blessing of our family. I thank God for the golden thread of the Prayer Chain Ministry that has, along with other ministries, stood in the gap for individuals, situations and governments.

Moldova Ministries is another golden thread woven through the tapestry, which has been blessed of God in the salvation of precious souls and in bringing relief to many. 'Remember your Creator now while you are young before the silver cord of life snaps...' (Eccles. 12:1, NLT). How often we prayed for the salvation of men and women and for our young people, that they may find Christ in their early years.

The other primary colours remind me of many other blessings God has woven through my life, the privilege of travelling and sharing the gospel in many countries. The men and women of God I have been privileged to know and serve with, the dear friends who have constantly prayed for us and encouraged us in our ministries.

A dear lady I worked beside in my first job, when I was sixteen years old, gave me a copy of this poem, which I have never forgotten.

> Behind my life the weaver stands,
> And works his wondrous skill.
> I leave it in his all wise hands,
> And trust his perfect will.

Should mystery enshroud his plan,
And my short sight be dim,
I will not try the whole to scan,
But leave each thread to him.
Often he weaves sorrow
And I, in foolish pride,
Forget he sees the upper
And I, the under side.

Not till the loom is silent,
And the shuttles cease to fly,
Will God unroll the canvas,
And explain the reason why
The dark threads are as needful,
In the weaver's skillful hands,
As the threads of gold and silver
In the pattern he has planned.

When grey threads mar life's pattern,
And seem so out of line,
Trust the Master Weaver
Who planned the whole design,
For in life's choicest patterns
Some dark threads must appear
To make the rose threads fairer
The gold more bright and clear.

The pattern may be intricate,
And hard to understand,
But trust the Master Weaver
And his steady guiding hand,
He knows, he loves, and he cares
Nothing this truth can dim,
He gives his very best to those
Who leave the choice to him.

I love the second verse because it reminds me that the loom is still working, and God is still weaving. But inevitably the time will come when the loom will be silent and I will be at home with the Lord. Only then I will fully understand all the way he has led me. The dark threads will be explained, although I'm not too concerned about the whys and wherefores of them, as I know that they were all for my good and for his glory.

An old couple lived in the country and they had an unpredictable grandfather clock. One night it chimed ten, eleven, twelve, thirteen times and kept going! So they wakened up and listened as it chimed on and on. Finally, the old man said to his wife, 'What time is it anyway?' She replied, 'I'm not sure, but I can tell you this, it's later than it's ever been before!' There's a lesson there. As we view the media and the newspapers, and relate them to the Word of God, we should realise that it's later than it's ever been before. It could be that we are living in the age when the Lord Jesus Christ will return to take his church home to be with him. In the light of this, how are we living as believers?

I'm reminded of a story I read in UCB's *Word for Today*. 'President Eisenhower was holidaying in Denver and he was told about a six-year-old boy, named Paul Haley, who was dying of an incurable cancer. Paul had one great dream – some day to meet the President of the United States. "Let's go see him", the President said to one of his aids. So they drove over to the boy's house. The flags on the bumper were flying as the big black limousine rolled up. Out stepped the President with his bodyguards and knocked on the door. Paul's father answered, wearing old jeans, a grubby shirt and a full day's growth on his beard. "Can I help ya?" he asked. The President responded, "Is Paul here? Tell him the President of the United States would like to meet him." Thrilled, little Paul Haley walked around his father's legs and stood looking up into the face he admired most. The President kneeled down, hugged him, and took him out to sit in the presidential limousine. Before they said goodbye they shook hands, then just as suddenly as he appeared, he left. The neighbours still talk about that day. But one man was not entirely happy about it, that was Paul's dad, Donald Haley, who said, "I'll never forget standing there in those old jeans, a dirty shirt and a grubby beard to meet the President of the United States. If only I'd known he was coming."

One day, and it may be sooner than we think, someone much more important than the President of the United States will suddenly appear as he promised. The 'Lord himself will descend from heaven with a shout, with the voice of the archangel, and with the trumpet of God. And the dead in Christ will rise first. Then we who are alive and remain shall be caught up together with them in the clouds to meet the Lord in the air. And thus we shall always be with the Lord' (1 Thess. 4:16-17, NASB). May I ask you, dear reader, a personal question? Will you be ready for the promised return of the Saviour when he comes for those who have made him Lord and Saviour?

A few weeks after the Billy Graham Mission at Parkhead, Glasgow (1991) when I had the privilege of being Prayer Co-ordinator, there was, for a few days, a follow-up conference held in Stirling University for church leaders. I will never forget the very challenging message given by the Rev. George McLeod. He said, 'I simply argue that the cross be raised again at the centre of the market place as well as on the steeple of the church. I am recovering the claim, that Jesus was not crucified in a cathedral between two candles; but on a cross between two thieves; on a town garbage heap, at a crossroads of politics so cosmopolitan that they had to write his title in Hebrew, Latin and in Greek. At the kind of place where cynics talk smut, and thieves curse and soldiers gamble because that is where he died, and that is what he died about, and that is where Christ's men ought to be and what God's people ought to be about.'

These words were a challenge to me then and still move me now. Jesus is still looking for men and women who will stand with him in the marketplace or even, if he asked, on a garbage heap. It's later than it has ever been before. It's decision time!

Perhaps you, like me, can look back over your lives and think of the many decisions you were called to make. To those of us who follow Jesus Christ, to decide to be obedient to the will of God is one of the most important decisions of our lives. In 1979/81 God took Peter and I through a very dark patch in our Christian lives. He taught us much about prayer and we emerged more mature. Out of that experience the ministry that I led for over twenty-five years was born of God.

At that time I had to make a decision to accept the challenge and trust God to equip me for the task of leading The Telephone Prayer Chain Ministry or to say no and walk away. I chose the former. I knew nothing about leadership or how to organise a prayer ministry. **But God** knew and that decision changed my life and I entered into the greatest adventure I could ever have known.

Over my lifetime I have made it a habit to underline and date in my Bible, any text which has touched my life, or jumped out at me significantly, one such verse was Isaiah 54:2, marked on the 14th May 1989. 'Enlarge the place of your tent, stretch out the curtains of your dwellings, spare not; Lengthen your cords, and strengthen your pegs' (NASB). Marked beside the text are the words, 'What Lord?'

I stand in awe and give thanks to God who would take someone like me and allow me the privilege of serving him. Like Nehemiah I can say that the 'good hand of my God was on me'. I pray that you will see beyond Jessie McFarlane. I am only a sinner, saved by God's wonderful amazing grace. I have told my story in order that you can see how God can take anyone who is obedient and available and make them capable of being used for his glory. Had I not been obedient all these years ago I would have missed so much.

I have had the privilege of meeting many wonderful people, who live in a completely different world from me in so many ways. Some have been like ships that pass in the night, others are still good friends. All of them have had an impact on my life. But the greatest impact ever made was when I met Jesus Christ. For over sixty-six years I have proved him to be all that he has promised in his Word, and he's not finished yet! My prayer and desire is that this account of a journey with God will be a blessing and encouragement to you. You may be finding life difficult right now, maybe you're in that dark tunnel, in the Refiner's fire, **but God** has plans for you.

Christian Focus Publications
publishes books for all ages

Our mission statement –

STAYING FAITHFUL

In dependence upon God we seek to impact the world through literature faithful to His infallible Word, the Bible. Our aim is to ensure that the Lord Jesus Christ is presented as the only hope to obtain forgiveness of sin, live a useful life and look forward to heaven with Him.

REACHING OUT

Christ's last command requires us to reach out to our world with His gospel. We seek to help fulfil that by publishing books that point people towards Jesus and help them develop a Christ-like maturity. We aim to equip all levels of readers for life, work, ministry and mission.

Books in our adult range are published in three imprints:

Christian Focus contains popular works including biographies, commentaries, basic doctrine and Christian living. Our children's books are also published in this imprint.

Mentor focuses on books written at a level suitable for Bible College and seminary students, pastors, and other serious readers. The imprint includes commentaries, doctrinal studies, examination of current issues and church history.

Christian Heritage contains classic writings from the past.

Christian Focus Publications Ltd,
Geanies House, Fearn, Ross-shire,
IV20 1TW, Scotland, United Kingdom.
www.christianfocus.com